# THE NOONDAY
# DEMON

By the Author

The Passion as Story / *The Plot of Mark*

# THE NOONDAY DEMON

RECOGNIZING AND CONQUERING
THE DEADLY SIN OF SLOTH

JOHN N. BLACKWELL

A *Crossroad* Book
The Crossroad Publishing Company
New York

The Crossroad Publishing Company
16 Penn Plaza, 481 Eighth Avenue
New York, NY 10001

Printed in the United States of America

The text type is 11.5/15 Goudy Oldstyle. Display type is Mason and Gill Sans.

**Library of Congress Cataloging-in-Publication Data**

Blackwell, John N.
    The noonday demon : recognizing and conquering the deadly sin of sloth / John N. Blackwell.
        p.   cm.
    "A Crossroad book".
    Includes bibliographical references.
    ISBN 0-8245-2136-6 (alk. paper)
    1. Laziness.  I. Title.
BV4627.S65B57 2004
241′.3 – dc22
                                                        2004000734

1  2  3  4  5  6  7  8  9  10        10  09  08  07  06  05  04

With joyful gratitude
I dedicate these pages to
Nancy, Jaime, and David,
my family of reflection,
whose love is imprinted on
every page of this book

# Contents

# Beyond Malaise

*Something less than faith will do. Faith is finding, but mere seeking overcomes sloth. For seeking becomes finding, and finding becomes joy, and joy overcomes sloth.*

— Peter Kreeft, *Back to Virtue*

THE TEAM GATHERED for our monthly meeting. We were planning a celebration. It would represent the climax of several years of planning and hard work to renew a gathering of people that had somehow lost its vitality.

The chair began the meeting by leading us in devotions. What he did was simple: he played an audiocassette tape. It consisted of a talk given by a woman who helped lead a retreat that the chair had attended the week before our meeting. He had recorded the talk himself.

I will never forget the woman's words. We all sat spellbound as she talked about the way we pray. She asked, what if instead of asking God for things, or trying to secure God's blessing on matters we had already decided, we were to ask, "God, would you give me a hunger for you? Would you draw me closer to you? Would you make me more prayerful?"

I was completely captivated. The words she spoke were self-authenticating. I was hearing the Voice of the Genuine, and I knew it deep in my soul. I had never prayed like she was suggesting. But her words rang true. I couldn't get her thoughts out of my head. I kept wondering, over and over: What would it mean for my life to pray that prayer? Would I somehow change? At the conclusion of her talk, the chairperson turned off the tape. A spontaneous silence gently held the group. We sat together enjoying the communion of souls. To conclude our devotions, the chair led us in prayer.

He then turned to the subject of our keynote speaker. We had been struggling together as a team to name the right speaker for our celebration. Someone had suggested a particular high profile speaker with good name recognition. Although we were not all thrilled about the name suggested, we finally had consented and given the chair the green light to explore the possibility.

The chair reported to us that he had contacted the man we were inviting to speak. He told us that the man wanted a $15,000 honorarium for his talk, plus two first-class plane tickets. Our entire budget for the celebration was $15,000, so financial considerations alone precluded this speaker. We were back to square one.

The group members looked at each other. We said, "Now what?" After a few moments of silence, I pointed to the cassette player and said, "What about her?"

The group lit up. The chair said that the idea sounded good to him. He left the room to go to a telephone. Within fifteen minutes, he had her consent. The woman's name is Paula D'Arcy. Paula became the keynote speaker for our celebration. Her talks were the beginning of what for me became a long spiritual journey of reflection.

I wish that I could say the changes were instant. They weren't even rapid. Not only would they be slow in coming, but in many respects I am not even close to where I believe I should be spiritually. But Paula more than launched me on my way.

Around the same time, another mentor entered my life somewhat miraculously. A friend whom I completely trusted approached me with a book. He gave it to me; it was a gift. His only words were, "Wait till you read this!" The book was entitled *The American Hour*. The author was an Englishman. His name is Os Guinness.

I grew to understand that Sloth is a kind of sleeping *sickness* that includes indifference, apathy, and joylessness.

At the time, while my spiritual life was in disarray, my intellectual life wasn't much better. To put it bluntly, I was intellectually arrogant. I was quite critical and skeptical as a thinker. I loved dissection and analysis. I also relished exposing and destroying the flaws in other people's thinking. But I was clueless as to the way my arrogance affected others. In retrospect, I had an inflated sense of my own importance and competence. My intellectual arrogance included a kind of heady oblivion. And I was for the most part *indifferent* and *apathetic* with regard to the impact my life had on others. But there was a problem with my indifference and apathy, though I didn't realize it at the time. They were creating a kind of malaise in my soul. I had become rather joyless and ungrateful. I had not only lost whatever enthusiasm I had for my life and vocation, I was just beginning to realize that much of the enthusiasm I had lost was driven by my Pride and my hunger for recognition and respect. The truth is that I was closing my eyes to my own indifference, ignoring its impact on others, and failing in my efforts to cope with a barely identifiable melancholy.

With the gift of the book came the gift of beginning to recognize an arrogance to which I had been closing my eyes. Os Guinness was presenting ideas that I had long rejected. The impact of his ideas and arguments was intellectually compelling, just as Paula's talks were self-authenticating.

Both Os and Paula had begun to identify a kind of malaise that was somehow undermining or even debilitating me spiritually. It was something I had only barely sensed. I knew it was there, but I was not entirely certain what it was. But as one thing so often leads to another, books by Os Guinness led me to other writings, some of which were on the Seven Deadly Sins — Pride, Envy, Wrath, Sloth, Avarice, Gluttony, and Lust. One of those — Sloth — is the subject of these essays. This Deadly Sin provided me with a way to understand the malaise that had poisoned so much of my life for so many years. I discovered that Sloth is not mere laziness. It isn't what we mean by *taking it easy,* or even *taking a nap.* I was to learn that it is much deeper than that. I grew to understand that Sloth is a kind of sleeping *sickness* that includes indifference, apathy, and joylessness. Sloth involves ignoring what is good, true, and beautiful. It includes apathy toward others — their dignity, their circumstances, and their feelings. And it includes joylessness, even in the face of extraordinary goodness and love. This joylessness all too often gives way to despair over God's purposes, plans, and willingness to love and help us in ways we cannot even imagine.

The gift that I received from Paula D'Arcy and Os Guinness involved both reassurance and challenge. These are gentle souls. I will never forget a telephone conversation with Os, where he impressed on me the grace of God that ever helps us on our journey.

Alongside his reassurance, he offered a kind challenge that at first intrigued me and later came to haunt me: Would I consider living before the Audience of One? In other words, what would it mean to begin to live before God? What would it mean to make God the primary audience of my life?

If Os put the bee in my bonnet, Paula began to show me the way. When I listened to her talk, she was describing one of the lowest points in her life. She had lost her husband and daughter in an accident, which she alone survived, and she was pregnant. She was dealing with both gut-wrenching grief and preparing to give birth to her second child. Paula wanted so much to find God. What she did was to approach God with the heart and mind of a child. When she moved into her new apartment, the first thing she did was to have tea with God. She got out her teapot and cups and sat in her new living room with God. She sought God — simply and directly. She sought to know God *as God truly is.*

When Paula told that story, I was stunned. What could be more important than seeking the Genuine — with the direct simplicity of a child?

Paula's and Os's reassurances and challenges have never left me. They have never ceased to be the object of my reflections. They initiated my growing to understand the way in which my own Sloth had lured me to sleep. At the same time, they encouraged me to open my eyes to the joy of living in reflection.

# Joyless Indifference

*In the United States the difficulties are not a Minotaur or a
dragon — not imprisonment, hard labor, death, government
harassment, and censorship — but cupidity, boredom, slop-
piness, indifference. Not the acts of a mighty, all-pervading,
repressive government, but the failure of a listless public to
make use of the freedom that is its birthright.*

— Aleksandr Solzhenitsyn, Harvard commencement address, 1978

I T WAS THE MOST MISERABLE memorial service I have ever
attended. I also officiated. It wasn't the circumstances of
death that were the cause of the wretchedness; it was the life
of the deceased. This funeral represents the only time in my
career in which the daughter of the deceased instructed me
merely to read the ritual. "Please don't say anything about him.
There is nothing good to be said, and reflecting on his life in
a eulogy would be completely undignified. Just read the ritual.
That is all."

Why were these her instructions? There was no malice involved. The woman was not wishing to degrade her father in
some way. But she was not willing to sugarcoat the truth, to
pretend that the way he lived his life was acceptable.

And what was it that was so unacceptable? It had to do with
her father's calculated cruelty. Where to begin? His bigotry is
one place to start. This man despised black people. He was
once run out of Corpus Christi, Texas, for seizing a black man,

tying the man to the back of his car, and then dragging him through the town. After this man married, he had numerous adulterous affairs. The first was on his honeymoon. And were that not enough, he was a terror to his wife. He was wont to beat her mercilessly, and he always landed his blows on the parts of her body that would be covered by her clothing. He also terrorized his family. He once burned the bottoms of his daughter's feet because he wanted to film her crying. He trained his dog with a cattle prod in an effort to hasten the puppy's obedience.

These reasons and more prompted this man's daughter to request that nothing be said about him at his funeral. This is why I merely read the ritual.

But my purpose for a brief review of this situation has less to do with the funeral and more to do with the question, What was happening in this man's life? What can we know about the contents of his character? How is it that one comes to live a life of chronic, calculated cruelty? The factors, of course, are legion. There are a host of variables that are valid and important. Some are psychological. Others pertain to his family of origin. Still others focus on moral upbringing, and so on. I wish to discount none of these. To get at the truth, the whole truth, and nothing but the truth almost always involves identifying a multiplicity of variables without which knowledge cannot be complete.

But as I pondered this horrific situation, I began to wonder if it were not possible to identify one factor or variable that somehow touched and affected all the other variables. Was there not something at large here that poisoned other components of this man's spirit or character? What struck me was this man's indifference. It was belligerent and sinister. The attitude that affected much of his behavior included sheer apathy. His blindness to the dignity of a fellow human being was aggressive.

As I reflected on this man's life, I remembered a short story that Shirley Jackson had published in the *New Yorker* on June 28, 1948. Her story was entitled "The Lottery." It begins on the morning of June 27. The day is sunny and clear. The entire episode is concluded before noon. A village of some three hundred residents is gathering for their annual lottery. Children are playing, gathering stones and placing them in a pile. Their parents are arriving. The atmosphere includes a nervous humorlessness as the mundane ritual unfolds. There are numerous comments on the traditions associated with the lottery, some of which have fallen by the wayside to the mild pseudo-consternation of some of the villagers. Absolutely no one is enthusiastic about the lottery, but neither does anyone seriously question its necessity. They simply carry it out. That is all.

The "winning" family is chosen by ballot. Each member of this family then takes a second ballot, producing one winner — Mrs. Tessie Hutchinson, wife of Bill and mother of three. When Mrs. Hutchinson is identified, she helplessly protests, "It isn't fair." And immediately all of the villagers, including her husband and children, stone her to death. That is the end of the story. The lottery is an annual ritual human sacrifice.

Many things about this ritual are shocking. Shirley Jackson is a masterful storyteller. The characters in the story are concerned that they get the lottery over before noon so they won't be late for lunch. They pay attention to the smoothness of the stones. Some regret that certain ceremonies that used to accompany the ritual have fallen by the wayside. But they have at least remembered to use stones. The characters grin faintly as they execute the ritual. But *they never seriously question or reflect on what they are doing.* They never ask, "Is this right? Is this necessary? Should we be doing this? Is there anything in my neighbor or family member that merits a lottery of human sacrifice?" There are no serious protests or reservations. Neither are there any expressions of grief. The characters exhibit no reasoning. Not once do they follow their hearts or listen to their consciences. They simply get the ritual over with. They kill a fellow human being. That is all.

One of the reasons great literature is important to our humanity is that it enables us to recognize truth. Great literature provides the substance out of which we organize our imaginations so we can see. Shirley Jackson has given us the wherewithal to recognize the Deadly Sin of Sloth. These people are sleepwalking through a ritual that constitutes a direct attack on the fabric of our humanity. They do so *completely without reflection.* Their consciences are, as it were, anesthetized. Their indifference, if not absolute, is militant. These people are in a mindless fog, possessed by an apathy that is deceptively aggressive. This apathy is what produces the unwillingness to reflect. The lottery is a ritual of *mere* execution. It is completely divorced from meaning, reason, and understanding. It involves a willful oblivion to the preciousness of life and the sovereignty of human dignity. It is mere human sacrifice — mere killing — without any evidence of thought whatsoever.

This is the Deadly Sin of Sloth. By Sloth, I do not mean laziness. Sloth is not the ability to relax or occasionally to take it easy. The enjoyment of relaxation is not deadly. Deadly Sin is what gives birth to other sins — to additional sin. And by sin I don't mean what we typically call crime, though a lottery of human sacrifice is certainly that. The sin that Shirley Jackson's story compels us to recognize is a kind of betrayal —

the betrayal of life, the betrayal of our humanity. *We betray our humanity when we are willfully blind.* We betray our humanity when we refuse to reflect, when we fail to ask questions, when we never, ever ponder. Why is this? I believe that reflection and learning are at the heart of what it means to be human. We are most human when we are learning through reflection. We grow in our humanity when we grasp and think about what we have been doing, what we are doing, or what we will be doing. *We grow in our humanity when, having thoughtfully pondered who we are and what we have been up to, we begin to allow changes to transform our consciousness and to dwell in our souls to the end that we become more human and live differently.* We become mindful of who we are, what we are doing, and the impact that what we do has on others. We begin to exercise forethought to live in ways that are good, helpful, and constructive.

One of the reasons great literature is important to our humanity is that it enables us to recognize truth.

Sloth is deadly inasmuch as it directly attacks and undermines human thoughtfulness and reflection. *Sloth is militant indifference, apathy, and thoughtlessness. Sloth is willful joylessness in the face of God's presence, purpose, and intentions.* Sloth involves humorless mindlessness with respect to life's dignity and preciousness. It poisons everything about us. Sloth is a fundamental betrayal of our humanity.

It was the wee hours of the morning. The time was 1:30 a.m. The place was a trailer park in a little town called Mesquite, located in Nevada near the Utah border. Two teenage siblings carrying butcher knives entered a mobile home, stabbed a toddler to death, and critically wounded her ten-year-old sister. A nineteen-year-old man surrendered to police just hours later, confessed to the attack, and implicated his sister.

Such behavior is nothing short of horrifying. It reminds us of school shootings and of snipers in Montgomery County, Maryland. How do we understand such a breathtaking, violent betrayal of life? I want to suggest that our understanding must include the Deadly Sin of Sloth. The offensive combination of indifference and apathy poison rebellion, causing some people to look down on others, allowing wrath to possess the human soul. This does not make violence inevitable, but it creates conditions that may lead to violence. Willful oblivion to goodness, human dignity, and the preciousness of life make degradation and killing all the more likely.

Thankfully, the Deadly Sin of Sloth is only half of the story. On December 11, 1979, Mother Teresa gave her Nobel Lecture. In it, she spoke of visiting nursing homes. She noticed that in these homes the residents have all the modern conveniences that anyone could want. But she also noticed that there were no smiles. The residents simply stared vacantly at the door. Curious about this, Mother Teresa spoke to one of the nuns working in the nursing home. Mother Teresa wondered aloud why there were no smiles, why they simply stared at the door. The Sister responded, "They are hoping that a son or daughter will come to visit them. They are hurt because they are forgotten."

What I would like to recognize is that Mother Teresa took notice. She was not indifferent. She wondered. She was curious. She saw. She pondered. She reflected. She also cared. Her compassion ran deep. Mother Teresa loved. And she ever expressed that love in her smile. *Curiosity leading to reflection is the answer to Sloth.* If Sloth is the problem, reflection is the solution. Reflection plows fallow soil in the human heart in which God sows the seeds that transform consciousness, producing fruit that lasts. We become more fully human. We live. We love. No longer do we sleepwalk through life. We live fully and completely in the present.

Mother Teresa reported a time when she witnessed a woman who had been transformed through reflection. A man had reported to Mother Teresa the hunger of a Hindu family with eight children. They had not eaten for days. The man pled with Mother Teresa: "Do something." Mother Teresa immediately took rice to the family. "I saw the children. Their eyes were shining with hunger."

When the woman received the rice, she divided it into two parts and immediately left her home. In a short while she returned. Mother Teresa asked the woman, "Where did you go?" The woman had taken the rice to a neighbor. It was a Muslim family. They were just as hungry as the Hindu woman and her children.

That woman was aware. She was completely mindful. She knew that her own hunger reflected the hunger of her neighbor. Her own hunger in no way rendered her indifferent. She was completely thoughtful and full of compassion. She loved.

My hope is that the pages that follow will help you to recognize and understand Sloth. I also hope that what follows will help you on your wonderful journey of thoughtful reflection. It is a journey well worth making.

# The Noonday Demon

*I make an absolute distinction between those who strive with all their might to learn and those who live without troubling themselves or thinking about it.* — Blaise Pascal, *Pensées*

**H**E STOOD THERE TRANSFIXED. He was mesmerized, filled with wonder. There was nothing particularly remarkable about the sight. It barely merited notice. Or at least, so I would think. The sight was as barren as it was ordinary. It was a tree in winter — dry, leafless. Yet he stood there, captivated, drinking it all in.

It was an epiphany for him. He found himself not only overcome, but overflowing with an awakening — a realization that in the not too distant future this bare tree would be in full leaf. It would bear fruit. It would become a thing of sheer beauty.

The year was 1666. His name was Nicholas Herman of Lorraine. He was eighteen years old. And right then, right there, Nicholas Herman resolved to understand the power he sensed in that tree. He wanted to discover that same power in his own life. Soon after, he was admitted into a monastery as a lay brother. Nicholas Herman became a barefooted Carmelite monk. He took the name Brother Lawrence.

Brother Lawrence's remarkable insight stunned me for its depth and simplicity. He stared at something that was not only common but also wasn't particularly worth looking at. In January each year, my wife, Nancy, and I go into our rose garden

21

and prune the roses. But we don't remain in the rose garden and stare at the thorny branches. We wait until spring when the roses are in bloom to gaze longer. But Brother Lawrence saw much more deeply than I ordinarily see. Brother Lawrence recognized — in the growth processes of a common tree — the Providence of God. The tree would be renewed. Flowers and fruit would appear. And it was all because the Power of God worked within the tree. Brother Lawrence also recognized that this same power worked within his own soul. And he resolved that he would never be separated from an awareness of that power.

For a monk, anything that distracted his attention from God, from God's providence, or from God's power was called Sloth. And for many of the earliest monks, Sloth became known as the *Noonday Demon*.

Brother Lawrence was a member of a long tradition called monasticism. And just as his own conversion began with his reflections on the *renewal* of the tree, so did the entire monastic tradition begin with the *quest for renewal*. The church has always stood in need of renewal. Sustaining faith has never been easy. The early Middle Ages were no exception. Much of the church's spiritual life was in disarray. And one of the causes was the debilitating persecutions that seemed unending. They were particularly intense during the reigns of Decius in the third century and Diocletian in the fourth. Decius was emperor of Rome from 249 to 251. He initiated the first systematic persecution of Christians. Decius blamed the Christians' worship of God for the domestic problems that Rome suffered. He reacted by issuing an edict in 251, demanding that all Romans sacrifice to the Roman gods and to the genius of the emperor. Failure to do so was punished with the confiscation of land, exile, torture, or death. Diocletian reigned from 303 to 311. Although he had practiced tolerance for Christians, he later extolled his own divinity. Diocletian then saw Christians as a threat. His solution was the extermination of all Christians. He launched a persecution of Christians that exceeded all other harassments in its brutality. If persecutions and terror weren't enough, the church also faced stifling economic difficulties. These challenges sent the church's spiritual life into a tailspin.

The church eventually found relief. Constantine became ruler of the West — Gaul, Spain, and Britain — in 306. And in 312 he led an army into Rome. On the way to Rome, Constantine converted to Christianity. When he became emperor of Rome in 313, Constantine protected Christians. Christianity became the religion of the state, and the church enjoyed success and prosperity. What I find interesting is that the enjoyment of privilege did little to boost the church's immunity to spiritual disarray. Now a part of the dominant culture, Christians reaped both wealth and success. What happened in response was that many Christians became lackadaisical about their faith. And the rise to power brought political strife within the church. Personal ambition all too often replaced a prayerful relationship with God. The result was that the church's faith was commonly in shambles.

It was in response to the deterioration of faith that some heard the call to renewal. And some separated from the dominant institution of the church in an effort to recapture the ideals of the Christian faith. They became Christianity's first monks. Many spent considerable time, if not all their time, in the desert. Some of their stories are far more eccentric than that of Brother Lawrence. But their eccentricity renders their purpose all the more clear. The first monk to receive historical recognition was St. Antony (ca. 251–356). Sometime around the year 270, Antony inherited the family farm in Egypt. But he also heard a sermon, and it stirred him. The preacher was reading from the nineteenth chapter of Matthew: "If you want to be perfect, go, sell your possessions and give to the poor, and you will have treasure in heaven." The words went right to Antony's heart. He responded by retreating into the desert. There he pursued God in solitude. His motive was to find God by doing exactly what the Gospel had directed. Antony became a full-time ascetic — a monk who spent all of his time in solitude. He sought to be single-minded in his pursuit of God. There, in the desert, Antony's goal was to become spiritually fit.

Another monk whose story is also somewhat eccentric is Simon Stylites (ca. 390–459). Simon went into the desert near Syria to live in isolation. There he constructed a pillar, on top of which he spent the last years of his life. From the top of the pillar, he would lower a bucket on a rope to exchange life's most meager essentials. Why such strange isolation? Simon wanted to devote his entire life to concentrating exclusively on God. Like Antony, he made giving undivided attention to God a full-time vocation.

Although most of the monks who were to follow the likes of Antony and Simon lived in communities, they still spent considerable time in solitude, and all devoted time to *reflection*. And they soon discovered that *sustained* reflection is easier said than done. Single-minded devotion to God is difficult at best. Reflection requires concentration, and concentration necessitates willpower. As with any worthy endeavor, the serious practitioner will inevitably face a trial. Monks of the early Middle Ages discovered that the serious challenge to sustained reflection was what they came to call "Sloth."

The monks saw Sloth as *the vice that plagued their vocation*. They characterized Sloth as a kind of sleeping sickness — a spiritual disease of torpor that lured the human spirit away from spiritual matters into vocational carelessness. Sloth represented a weakening of the human will. For many, this weakening began prior to their answering the call to a life in seclusion. Sloth had its beginnings in the temptations to sins of the flesh. Sustained Gluttony (the love of eating) and Lust (the love of sex) saturated, clouded, and weakened the human spirit and thought processes. One became increasingly vulnerable to diversions from the ideals of the faith. The soul became listless, anesthetizing the monks' ability to concentrate on Scripture and prayer.

For a monk, anything that distracted his attention from God, from God's providence, or from God's power was called Sloth. And for many of the earliest monks, Sloth became known as the *Noonday Demon*.

The monks of the Middle Ages learned that a life of solitude posed its own peculiar challenges — particularly for those monks who lived alone in the desert. They learned that the hour of noon posed the specter of temptation to lose focus on God and matters of the spirit. One man who became acutely aware of this problem was John Cassian. Cassian lived in the fifth century. He was a monastic reformer. Cassian spent considerable time studying monastic practices in Egypt. And in order to maintain a strong monastic tradition in the West, he imported ideas from Egypt. In 425, Cassian wrote *Instituta*. The purpose of this book was to help monks overcome the peculiar pitfalls that they faced. One problem in particular was the Deadly Sin of Sloth. Cassian pointed out that elder monks had begun to refer to Sloth as the *Noonday Demon*. The idea was simple. The solitary monk, facing stifling heat at midday, depended solely on his own inner resources of concentration. Sloth was the noonday sleeping sickness. It melted the monk's concentration, and it eroded his ability to love God with the full devotion that God's sovereign goodness merited. This early monastic understanding characterized Sloth as inducing a midday stupor of spiritual passivity and dejection. Its symptoms were laziness, despair, ennui, listlessness, melancholy, lethargy, torpor, or moral burnout.

The problem is that when we are spiritually numb, we become increasingly susceptible to a host of other sins, the best of which may be neglect, and the worst of which involve harm to others. These thoughtful monks, in other words, recognized that the consequences of Sloth could be deadly. That is why it came to be counted as a Deadly Sin.

When I looked at the early monk's ability to identify Sloth, I began to understand my own difficulties with concentrating on God and maintaining my own faith and prayer life. I was completely smitten by the prayer life of Brother Lawrence. I was in awe of his simplicity, his single-minded devotion, and his concentration. Brother Lawrence had learned to converse with God continually. He frequently nourished himself on high notions of the character of God. He wanted nothing more than to keep his faith alive. He sought to take God alone as the rule of his conduct. He avoided anything that was trivial; superficiality not only diverted attention from God but changed almost daily. He watched carefully over his passions; he trusted that God would always give him the light, understanding, direction, and willpower to deal with them. He counted times of spiritual dryness as a blessing: these were the times when God was testing the sincerity of his devotion. Brother Lawrence summarized his goal as the "Practice of the Presence of God."

When I wanted to set aside my own pursuit of the superficial and to know God more directly and intimately, I treasured Brother Lawrence because his directions were so simple. But I soon learned that simplicity doesn't necessarily guarantee ease. Push-ups and sit-ups are simple. But they still call for great commitment and willpower. And though a part of me wanted a *sustained* relationship with God, I soon learned that it was all too easy to become spiritually lazy. Worse, I discovered that this laziness effortlessly gave way to indifference. This indifference seemed to be the very problem that the monks of the early Middle Ages knew so well.

Still, Brother Lawrence provided all kinds of hope for this beginner. He knew all about Sloth. He was intimately familiar with the obstacles to knowing God directly. One thing in particular continues to help me. Brother Lawrence learned not to beat up on himself when he failed to give God his attention. Instead, Brother Lawrence learned to draw his consciousness back into the Presence of God gently and lovingly. He had the deepest respect for his own consciousness, but recognized that like a small child, consciousness must be brought along one step at a time, with great love. What Brother Lawrence discovered is that when he did so, God blessed him with the grace that he needed to draw back to God. And God then gave him the grace to withstand the Noonday Demon that worked so hard at undermining his love for God.

# THE ORDER
## OF LOVES

*Now he is a man of just and holy life who forms an unprejudiced estimate of things and keeps his affections also in strict control, so that he neither loves what he ought not to love, nor fails to love what he ought to love, nor loves that more which ought to be loved less, nor loves that equally which ought to be loved either less or more, nor loves that less or more which ought to be loved equally.* — Augustine, *On Christian Doctrine*

A S HE STOOD IN FRONT of a barren tree in 1666, Brother Lawrence saw the entire Providence of God in the tree. He recognized not only that in a few months the tree would be in leaf and bear fruit, but that the same power governing the tree was at work in his own soul. And he saw this because he was fully awake. He was looking with both eyes.

I had just finished reading Brother Lawrence when I imagined an earlier monk standing in front of the same tree. And it occurred to me that this other monk would see something similar to what Brother Lawrence saw. But because of his education and orientation to the world, the other monk would also see something else. And that something else was *order.*

This other monk's name was Augustine of Hippo (354–430). He was a great orator, philosopher, theologian, and bishop of the church. He was an original thinker, and he became one of the most influential Christian writers of all time. St. Augustine was the kind of sophisticated thinker who would see this barren tree as an expression and derivative of the order of God. For him, order was key. At the heart of the Christian life is what St. Augustine called "the order of loves." The idea of the order of loves is straightforward. It involves loving the right things and loving the right things rightly. *Sloth, on the other hand, makes us indifferent to order. Sloth undermines our ability to love the right things in the right way.*

Order. What is it? Where does this order come from? Order is one of those immeasurably profound terms. Order is profound because it is irreducible. Once you break it up, you no longer have order. It can take different forms. Or, to put it another way, order expresses itself in various ways. You would see this were you to investigate the Blackwell household. There are four of us. I have one wife, Nancy, and we have two grown children, Jaime and David. Nancy and David love for our home to be in order physically. Everything has its place. They love it when things are put away. Then, and only then, is everything in order. Jaime and I, on the other hand, *think* of ourselves as orderly. But you'd never know it by looking at where we have been. For Jaime and me the order is in our heads. That is where we organize our worlds; that is where we keep track of things. If Nancy enters a place where Jaime or I have been, she sees the aftermath of Hurricane Helga and becomes completely overwhelmed. As far as Jaime and I are concerned, such anxiety is needless. We know where everything is. And if we don't? Not to worry. Just ask Mom! As Shakespeare's Hamlet would say, "Ah, there's the rub."

What, then, is order? There are synonyms. They include words like "organization," "plan," "blueprint," and "recipe." But that we cannot necessarily define it with razor-sharp precision isn't really a problem. I'll assume that we pretty much know what we mean by order. We certainly know what chaos is!

Where does this order come from? St. Augustine's way of looking at the world is part of a tradition that goes all the way back to the beginning — to creation itself. It is well known that the Bible begins with a story of creation in Genesis 1. Perhaps less well known is the account of creation that is given in the eighth and ninth chapters of Proverbs. The subject matter is order. And here, order is given a name. Her name is *Sophia.* The English word is "wisdom." The writer is quoting Sophia; it is Sophia who speaks. She tells us that before God created the heavens and the earth, God created her. God's *first* act of creation was to create *order.* God could not have created the world without her. And having first created her, God then used her to create the heavens and the earth. And God did so by *delivering the cosmos from chaos to produce a world.* In fact, this is a foundational biblical understanding of the world. A world is a cosmos that God has delivered from chaos by means of order. World and order may not be synonymous, but they certainly go hand in glove. Biblically speaking, you cannot have a world without order.

This biblical understanding of order is remarkable for many reasons, not the least of which is that order is also a neces-sary condition for *life.* Erwin Schrödinger (1887–1961) was a Viennese-born physicist who spoke to the question, What is life? with profundity born of clarity and simplicity. He began his discussion by pointing to death: When something is dead, all motion comes to a standstill. What dies rapidly moves into a state of equilibrium — what scientists call maximum entropy. What is alive, on the other hand, does something that the dead cease to do — it exchanges energy with the environment. This exchange of energy is called metabolism. *Life consists of drinking orderliness from the environment.* What is alive in one way or another sucks, drinks, eats, digests, assimilates, and uses order. The order that can be assimilated is usable energy.

There is more. What is alive also has the ability to discharge chaos in the form of its own waste products. Moreover, any living organism cannot survive on a diet of its own waste. This would prove too toxic for the living organism's sustenance. The products of waste, for the living organism, have crossed the line distinguishing chaos from order. A diet of its own waste ultimately poisons the living organism's ability to drink orderliness from the world. This leads to death. Unlike death, life goes on doing something. And it is the orderliness of the world that is responsible for life. Life comes from life inasmuch as life ultimately consists of the drinking in of orderliness.

Schrödinger made another simple, but important, observation. This order by which God created the heavens and the earth is *aperiodic.* I recognize that "aperiodic" is not a word that most people use in everyday conversation. But like order, it is a simple concept and easy to understand. Aperiodic order is the opposite of periodic order. Periodic order is repetitive. A drumbeat that is repeated over and over and over and over may be said to be periodic. A checkerboard or a chessboard is periodic. The pattern is obvious, and the pattern is clear. The pattern is also monotonous; it *merely* repeats. Ultimately, mere repetition is uninteresting and ultimately puts us to sleep! Aperiodic order, on the other hand, has *direction.* It is the order that moves toward a particular *result.* For example, my wife and I love our rose garden. And the rose garden moves toward a goal. Nancy and I cut the rose bushes back in January. It's called pruning. We also feed the rose bushes with fertilizer. When pruned, the rose bushes aren't much to look at, but the result is well worth waiting for. By spring the bushes have produced a unique beauty, which includes stunning color and delicious fragrance. And that is because the order is aperiodic; it moves toward a particular *result*. The same is true of a human being. What begins as ovum and sperm develops into a person of priceless, incalculable sovereignty and self-evident, irreplaceable dignity. This dignity comes from the cosmic order that ultimately sustains the person's life.

Sloth is the Deadly Sin that attacks our desire to know God and the order that God created. Sloth makes us indifferent to the form that God wants the world and our relationships to take. Sloth makes us indifferent to order and unable to love.

Just as dignity comes from the order of the world, the order of the world comes from God. And both St. Augustine and the writer of Proverbs understood that because God is the creator of both aperiodic order in general and human dignity in particular, ideas such as justice and righteousness derive from a solid foundation — the order of the world. That is why St. Augustine emphasized the importance of the *order* of loves — loving the right things in the right way.

To love things in the right way, one needs to be awake — alert and fully aware. That is the function of the proverbs that follow the story of the creation of Sophia and the world. All of these remarkable sayings are, in one way or another, related to creation. They are *expressions* of order; they are vital to *understanding* the fruits of order.

One of the problems with understanding order is that by itself, order is completely abstract. For it to be meaningful, it needs flesh and blood. That's why the writer of Proverbs gives order a name — *Sophia*. That is also why all those sayings follow. They show us order and creation in action, with real live people. They show us different aspects of what it means to be wise. They teach us how to imagine loving the right people in the right way. The proverbs, in other words, are designed to make us wise, just, and righteous.

To accomplish this task, several of these sayings portray people who are *indifferent* to order. They are the lazy and the scoffers. They are the apathetic. They are the ones who, in one way or another, are indifferent to life, order, and world. The lazy are like a door that swings on its hinges. They merely turn over in their beds. They are oblivious to the order of the world, to the things that matter most in life. And the scoffers, because of their indifference, are beyond rebuke. They cannot be corrected. They are so set in their ways that they have made themselves unable to learn. And because they cannot learn, they will never be wise. Being unwise, they are less than fully human.

This understanding of order is at the heart of St. Augustine's understanding of the world. He was vitally interested in teaching us how to love the right things in the right way. And for this to happen, the Christian had to be *in tune* with the order of the world. We have to know not only the form God intends for the world to take; we need to know something about the kinds of relationships God intends for the world. Those relationships all come from God's order.

Sloth is the Deadly Sin that attacks our desire to know God and the order that God created. Sloth makes us indifferent to the form that God wants the world and our relationships to take. Sloth makes us indifferent to order and unable to love.

At the heart of St. Augustine's understanding of order and Sloth is his recognition that the Slothful rarely love the right things in the right way, precisely because they are so indifferent. He recognized that a key symptom of Sloth can be seen in the person who loves sinners *because they are sinners* instead of loving them because they are children of God.

Not long ago, as I was preparing to lead Vespers, I received word about a terrible accident that took place in Los Angeles. An eighty-six-year-old man drove his car at high speed through a farmers' market. At the time of this writing, ten people were dead and at least forty-five were injured. With millions of others, my heart went out to the victims, their families, all who were helping, and the eighty-six-year-old man himself.

In alluding to this accident, I do so with the greatest respect. I believe that God calls us to love all of the people involved, including the eighty-six-year-old driver of the car. I believe that God calls us to love them all deeply — to weep with them — because they are children of God. They are all priceless expressions of life. Each bears a unique dignity.

By the same token, God does *not* call us to love a man *because* he drove his car through a farmers' market and killed people. That kind of perverse love — being attracted to someone *because* he is a sinner — is the fruit of Sloth, as St. Augustine teaches us. To illustrate it another way, it is one thing to love Eric Harris and Dylan Klebold, the boys who perpetrated atrocities at Columbine High School, because they are children of God. It would be quite another to be attracted to them because of what they did. One act is an expression of genuine love; the other is the fruit of Sloth — militant indifference and apathy — which is clearly evil and in violation of the order of the world.

This gives us another window on the reason the church came to understand Sloth as a Deadly Sin. If I am so indifferent to the preciousness and dignity of order and life that I am attracted to and love people because they kill or injure, my own indifference creates the internal character that makes it possible, and even probable, that I will do likewise. Those who admire an Osama bin Laden, who was responsible for the terrorist attacks on the World Trade Center on September 11, 2001, are the kinds of people who are likely to imitate him. Similarly, those who admire Timothy McVeigh, who bombed the federal building in Oklahoma City, are also candidates for taking deadly action. Sloth is a Deadly Sin because it creates the internal conditions that ignore God's order of the world and make it more likely that one will kill in cold blood.

# "I Couldn't Care Less"

*Relaxing is not Sloth. The person who never relaxes is not a saint, but a fidget.* —Peter Kreeft, *Back to Virtue*

O NE OF MY FAVORITE PLACES to write is in Wales. It's called St. Deiniol's Residential Library. The library is located in the little town of Hawarden, just south of Chester. It's a place devoted solely to Christian learning. You go to St. Deiniol's to read and write, to eat and rest. Occasions for conversation are also a regular feature at St. Deiniol's. In addition to three meals, the library serves tea three times a day. Pastors and scholars visit quietly. The topic of conversation almost always begins with questions about what one is there to work on.

Just after Easter 2003, I spent a couple of weeks there for the sole purpose of writing the first draft of this manuscript. When I first arrived, I was the only American in the place. When people asked what I was working on, I would tell them, "a book on Sloth." Without exception, my inquirer expressed surprise. "It seems like a strange book for an American to write. You Americans are so *busy*. Your lives are *filled* with activity. You put us Brits to shame!"

I was not surprised at the response of my British friends, especially when I considered the penance for Sloth that Dante prescribes in his "Purgatory" (Book 2 of *The Divine Comedy*). The penance is *ceaseless activity*. The souls in Dante's Purgatory are running. And that is because Dante saw the virtue appropriate for purging Sloth to be Zeal. In order to cultivate Zeal, the Slothful are made to labor. They are given no verbal prayers to utter. Their prayers consist of perpetual labor.

Many of us think of Sloth as inactivity. It is no secret that some who are Slothful might just as well be singing, "Nearer, my pew, to Thee," if not "Nearer, my couch, to Thee." Understandably, some people assume that if you are *busy* — especially to the point of being frantic — you cannot possibly be vulnerable to Sloth.

Dorothy Sayers saw otherwise. Sayers was a distinguished translator and interpreter of Dante. She also wrote insightfully on the Seven Deadly Sins. Sayers was quick to recognize that Sloth is not the same as idleness. As Peter Kreeft, to wit, has written, "Relaxing is not Sloth. The person who never relaxes is not a saint, but a fidget." Sayers recognized that mere busyness can be a symptom of Sloth: "It is one of the favorite tricks of this Sin to dissemble itself under the cover of a whiffling activity of body. We think that if we are busily rushing about and doing things, we cannot be suffering from Sloth. And besides, violent activity seems to offer an escape from the horrors of Sloth. So the other sins hasten to provide a cloak for Sloth: Gluttony offers a whirl of dancing, dining, sports, and dashing very fast from place to place to gape at beauty-spots which, when we get to them, we defile with vulgarity and waste. Covetousness rakes us out of bed at an early hour in order that we may put pep and hustle into our business; Envy sets us to gossip and scandal, to writing cantankerous letters to the papers, and to the unearthing of secrets and scavenging of dustbins; Wrath provides (very ingeniously) the argument that the only fitting activity in a world so full of evildoers and evil demons is to curse loudly and incessantly . . . while Lust provides that round of dreary promiscuity that passes for bodily vigor. But these are all disguises for the empty heart and the empty brain and the empty soul of Acedia." And this is what Sayers wrote in 1941.

Why all the whiffling activity? We rush from here to there. While doing one thing, we are planning the next. We rarely sit still. Our lives are an obsession of chronic hurry. Is there a reason for the way in which we so frantically burn calories? The French philosopher Blaise Pascal (1623–62) saw the life of ceaseless activity as a symptom of *willful indifference*. And just what are we indifferent to? Pascal's answer has to do with *matters of eternal consequence — the immortality of the soul*. People willfully ignore the one matter that is inescapably vital to each and every soul. This is Pascal's understanding of the sin of Sloth — willful indifference, leading us to ignore the things that matter most in life. The Slothful simply cannot be troubled with matters pertaining to eternity. The question that Pascal answers is, How do we pull off this studious neglect? His answer? *Through endless diversions.* Whatever it takes to preoccupy or otherwise entertain ourselves will do. As long as we can avoid asking, "Who am I? Why am I here? Where am I going?" we'll be fine. But for that to happen, we require one diversion after another — diversions ad infinitum. It is difficult to imagine a more tragic result than sheer indifference to the loss of our being. "What does it profit us to gain the whole world if we lose our souls?"

It was Dorothy Sayers who recognized that one of the ways we practice indifference is in our insistence on absolute tolerance. For many of us, tolerance is the buzzword. We must be tolerant of anything and everything. But the problem that Sayers identified is that a person who is tolerant of everything will finally stand for nothing. When we stand for nothing, we become vulnerable to believing just about anything at one time or another, with complete disregard for its truth or falsehood, its constructiveness or destructiveness. Instead, we mindlessly substitute taste (our own) for truth (which we find distasteful). Sayers describes a slogan that some of us wear as a badge of honor: "I couldn't care less." When overcome by Sloth, we not only have nothing to die for, we have nothing to live for. G. K. Chesterton captured this spirit of stupor in his pithy words about the Christian faith. "Christianity has not so much been tried and found wanting as found difficult and left untried." And the reason is sheer indifference, linking diligence to our diversions and tenacity to our tolerance, all of which lays the groundwork for evil as the offspring of effortlessness. If we are tolerant of everything, then in the end, anything goes.

What happens if the slogan by which I live is "I couldn't care less?" Dorothy Sayers recognized that when possessed by Sloth we become paralyzed by dread, morbid introspection, and despair. Why is this? It is because we don't deeply care about goodness. Because we don't give lots of attention to the possibilities of goodness, we almost never feel genuine joy. This means that each and every day will be one of fear and dread. When we look inward, we find few inner resources to help us resist temptation. It's as though our spiritual immune system is debilitated. When we have almost no resistance to evil, we end up in despair. The results can be terrifying, unless we can succeed in manufacturing at least *some* indifference to despair.

St. Augustine wrote extensively on all kinds of sin, including Sloth. He recognized a similar result when we become militantly *careless*. When we refuse to welcome, ponder, and enjoy goodness, we sentence ourselves to "enjoying" only evil. We then run the danger of making evil our obsession. It is one thing to be wary of evil — "wise as serpents," as Jesus would say; it is quite another thing to become fascinated and mesmerized by evil. The problem is that this intrigue strengthens our indifference to goodness and renders us all the more vulnerable to evil. St. Augustine put it succinctly. Sin is the punishment for sin, he would say. And since Sloth is *sadness of good and the joy of evil,* the Slothful will simply reap more Sloth. That is what leads to hardness of heart.

Busyness is the fruit of the Tree of Indifference, and we have made this fruit the staple of our diets. Rush and hurry have become the forms that Sloth often takes in the twenty-first century. By our busyness, we refuse God's goodness.

Geoffrey Chaucer (1343–1400) was an English poet who wrote about all of the Deadly Sins in *The Canterbury Tales.* He saw this indifference to goodness leading to extravagant sorrow and fear. The problem Chaucer recognized is that when we reject goodness, we make ourselves immune to joy. This produces that debilitating despair, even over the possibility of God's infinite mercy. Chaucer knew that God's expectations for humans were high. He saw this as completely necessary: high expectations befit the dignity wherewith God has created humans, male and female, in his own image. For God to expect anything less than our best would require the Creator to demean his own creation. But even with high expectations, Chaucer fully recognized the grace of God. He knew that God's human creatures, being human, are bound to fail from time to time. And yet, when we fail, God's goodness remains steadfast. God pours forth mercy and forgiveness, even as he draws us back into the fold. The problem is our refusal to recognize this. *When overcome by Sloth, we reject God's mercy in favor of despair and sadness.* The sadness of the Slothful isn't the natural, healing sadness that accompanies loss. It is a chronic, nagging, morbid sadness. And a morbid sadness that is the fruit of Sloth reduces us to severe idleness. Protracted despair and sadness produce a debilitating inertia. The result is paralysis of will. In *The Canterbury Tales,* Chaucer writes, "Sloth has no ... diligence; it does everything sadly and with peevishness, slackness, and false excusing, and with slovenliness and unwillingness. ... " Sloth is deadly inasmuch as it "will endure no hardship nor any penance."

The irony is that we Americans often use our busyness as a means to avoid hardship or penance. Indulging in a whirlwind of diversions, we diligently evade reflecting on the things that matter most in life. Busyness is the fruit of the Tree of Indifference, and we have made this fruit the staple of our diets. Rush and hurry have become the forms that Sloth often takes in the twenty-first century. By our busyness, we refuse God's goodness.

I AM BLESSED with thoughtful, respectful colleagues. We all have busy schedules. We even share an agreement that our schedules are too busy. But at least once a week, we sit together and reflect. We try to learn from each other, and often do. Instead of debating and trying to win arguments, we converse. We not only ask each other questions, we place questions and reflect together on each question posed. When it came to Iraq and Saddam Hussein, for example, we knew, before we ever opened our mouths, that the sparks would fly if each of us merely imposed his or her view. So what we did was ask, Who is responsible for Saddam Hussein? And what kinds of options are available to the responsible body? My colleagues — Jim,

Molly, Randy, Tom, Djalma, and Peggy — and I have learned that when we search for answers together, we balance our opinions with reverence for God, respect for human dignity, and our mutual commitment to goodness, truth, and beauty. We have found that this also helps us in our desire to practice a healthy tolerance for others, while avoiding the trap of becoming tolerant of actions that are wrong. We recognize that whereas we are committed to finding truth, none of us has a corner on truth.

One of my colleagues, Randy, is our youth minister. From him I have learned ways to reintroduce the spiritual discipline of reflection into our ministry. As a youth minister, Randy is confronted by a culture that Dorothy Sayers has identified as plagued by *whiffling activity*. So many young people rush from school to soccer to dance to swimming to baseball to gymnastics to piano lessons to the beach to homework, and on and on and on. This is quite different from the time when I grew up: We had a park. It was near our home, church, and school. It had rolling hills covered with grass and trees. I grew up in San Diego, where the weather is nice year-round. This meant that we kids could — and did — spend hours at the park. Much of that time involved merely lying on the grass, looking at the sky. What were we doing? Relaxing? Yes and no. We were also daydreaming, thinking, pondering, and reflecting. We took time. Sometimes we kids would lie there alone. Other times, we would visit quietly — talking to one another while we looked at the sky and clouds. We would, of course, get up and play football, baseball, and basketball. But sometimes we would just lie there and reflect. In retrospect, those long periods of quiet were essential to our growing up. We didn't know it at the time, but those meditative hours were at the heart of our humanity.

My friend Randy understands this. He is a master at leading retreats for young people. His very demeanor and ways of interacting with youths promotes this kind of reflection in their lives. Randy has recovered the lost art of *hanging out*. He is completely respectful of the busy lives that the young people live. But he also knows how to nudge them out of their busyness into a sacred place where they can ponder and visit — quietly, and with great joy. Randy is friend and mentor to many young people. What he does is quiet their spirits. He helps them to discover a rather large interior space with room for reflection. Internally, the young people discover something more of what it means to be fully human. The gift that Randy holds out to them is the possibility of transformation into people who take time to care — about their souls and the rest of the world.

# Abraham's Sloth

*Anyone who makes no mistakes in speaking is perfect, able to keep the whole body in check with a bridle.*

— James 3:2, NRSV

**W**ARTS AND ALL. That's the phrase we sometimes use when we read about someone whose unflattering qualities are not hidden from us. The Book of Genesis does that with Abraham. We call him the Father of Faith. We do so because he grew to trust God absolutely. But when the authors of Genesis wrote his story, they didn't hide Abraham's weaknesses. For my own efforts at growing, I have found this to be enormously comforting. The Father of Faith had his own personal obstacles to overcome.

The challenges that Abraham faced were formidable. The first has to do with a call. Abram (his name had not yet been lengthened) heard a Voice. The Voice gave a command: "Leave this place. Go to a place I will show you." Abram was given no road map. And I have found no evidence that the Voice told Abram ahead of time *where* he was going. The Voice simply said, "Follow my lead."

This initiated my reflections on the remarkable risk that Abram took from the get-go. Genesis gives no evidence that other people heard the Voice. And Abram himself would have had to trust that the Voice would continue to speak to him. That in itself was chancy. Did it ever occur to Abram that the

Voice might lead him halfway and then abandon him, speaking no more? To trust that the Voice would continue to speak was remarkable in and of itself.

I have the impression that the Voice completely inflamed Abram's consciousness. It must have been undeniably compelling. Abram would learn not only that the Voice would make promises, but that the Voice would make good on those promises. Eventually, not only would Abram learn, from experience, that the Voice was trustworthy, he would grow familiar with the Voice.

When Abram arrived at his destination, he built an altar. What is the significance of this? In Abram's day, one kindled a fire on an altar and sacrificed the first fruits of one's flock or herd. Why did Abram build an altar right away?

It seemed to me that his building an altar somehow reflected his experience of the Voice. Abram's experience of God resembled his experience of fire. Like fire, the Voice was insubstantial, but undeniably real. There is an inescapable ambiguity and even unpredictability with fire. It is both comforting and terrifying. It warms, but it also burns. And it cannot be controlled. Fire is, finally, unsupervised. If the flame is small — say, the flame of a candle — the fire can be blown out easily. But if the flame is large enough, wind can turn the flame into wildfire.

There seems to be a connection between Abram's experience of fire and his experience of God. His interaction with God was so profound, so transforming, so real, and so undeniable, that it merited preserving and even reproducing. So Abram built an altar, kindled a fire, and called upon the Name of the Lord.

Fire would have been the most vital, dramatic element in Abram's experience. It would have been the one most like God. And this God, whom Abram had heard, obeyed, and followed, merited Abram's frequent, if not ongoing, attention. I think that's the reason he built the altar — he found the Voice to be worthy of reflection. That's one of the reasons I am in awe of Abram.

But no sooner does Genesis finish with the awe-inspiring story of Abram answering God's call than the writer immediately turns to Abram's struggles. Abram and Sarai, his wife, were living in Canaan. Faced with the specter of a famine, they went to Egypt in search for food.

As they made their journey, Abram started getting nervous. His wife, Sarai, was beautiful. Abram started to imagine other men wanting Sarai — so much that he was sure they would kill him just to have her. Abram become so fearful that he asked Sarai to lie in order to save his skin. He asked her to tell the Egyptians that she was his sister.

Sarai did just that, and Abram sold his wife, Sarai, into Pharaoh's harem. This made it possible for Pharaoh to become physically intimate with Sarai, unwittingly committing adultery with her. Because of this, God cursed Pharaoh's house with plagues.

I recognize that Pharaoh's reaping plagues may seem a bit unfair to Pharaoh, especially when we consider that Abram was the one person who wasn't punished. After all, Pharaoh didn't realize that Sarai was married. Nevertheless, from the perspective of the writers of Genesis, Pharaoh was in violation of the sacred order whether he realized it or not. The writers of Genesis recognized that the sacred order of the universe, which includes the relationship between husband and wife, is objective and real, regardless of whether we recognize and acknowledge this.

But this does not prevent our recognizing that Abram was insensitive at best. He was also clearly cowardly. Abram was indifferent to what selling Sarai into Pharaoh's harem was doing to his own wife as well as to Pharaoh. Pharaoh made Abram a rich man. Abram, on the other hand, made Pharaoh and Sarai into adulterers, and Pharaoh suffered plagues for a sin he didn't realize he was committing.

What's going on here? And why do the writers of Genesis show us Abram not only at his best, but also at his worst? It seems that they recognize Abram as a real, live human being. It seems that his growth both in faith and in his relationship with Sarai and others was uneven at best. Like so many of us, Abram had his shortcomings. Abram suffered from many of the same human frailties and weaknesses that we do.

What the writers of Genesis have allowed us to discover is the struggle that Abram had in his relationships and actions — a struggle that was in part plagued by indifference and apathy, especially toward his wife. Hundreds of years later, the church would use a word for one of Abram's problems. The word is "Sloth." It refers to an insensitivity toward others that is so gross in character that it consists of indifference and apathy, which Abram is blind to in this case. Despairing of his own ability to save his own skin, Abram closes his eyes to the way that his efforts to save himself affect others. Abram's Sloth was deadly: it led him to betray both his own wife and the king of the nation that was serving as Abram's host in his time of need.

One of the reasons Abram's story is so poignant for me is that it helps me awaken to my own Slothful insensitivity to others, including my wife, Nancy. Many years ago, Nancy and I were struggling with our relationship. What I needed to learn was that a large part of our struggle was the fruit of my Sloth. I was far too indifferent to Nancy's feelings and the impact that my self-absorption made on her.

We came to a place where I was ready to listen. I was finally ready to *hear* her. I will confess that I was a bit scared; I was pretty sure that some of my behaviors and mannerisms were hard on her. One was related to my sense of humor. I love to laugh. I love kidding others. There is nothing wrong with this as long as I am sensitive to the impact I make on others. There are times that my humor can bring great joy to people or a situation. But there have also been countless times when my humor was a bit over the edge and out of control. And in the earlier years of our marriage, I loved not only teasing Nancy, but also making her the butt of my jokes. I thought I was so funny! Little did I know that on the inside, Nancy was dying a thousand deaths. I was so insensitive that I was clueless as to how much humiliation and heartache my humor was sometimes causing her.

By the grace of God, there came a time when I wanted to know how I truly affected my wife. And Nancy reached deep within her soul for the courage to disclose to me the impact that my misuse of humor made on her. I can only begin to convey how badly I felt as I began to recognize the rotten fruit of Sloth for which I alone was responsible. But Nancy's commitment to our marriage, along with her breathtaking patience, created a climate in which I was able to rouse myself from my self-absorption and apathy. She received me with grace, and her grace made it possible for me to begin to change.

I was able, for the most part, to go "cold turkey" on humor at Nancy's expense. Nancy responded with gratitude and encouragement for the changes I was trying to make. The challenge was that I had more to learn, more growing to do. I needed not only to change the way I used humor with Nancy, but I also needed to make changes with respect to my use of humor in general. I am a child of the 1960s. Much of the humor that we used when I was growing up was not only at the expense of others but also just plain inappropriate — not in the best of taste. Having learned what my humor was doing to Nancy, I needed to discover what my humor was doing to others. The recognition and changes would be slow in coming. I had to learn that I have a motor mouth, to which I had also been indifferent. I habitually shot from the lip. All too often, the words were out of my mouth long before I had taken my self-control out of neutral. I found myself wishing that I could give my motor mouth a major overhaul with an automatic pause button that would stop inappropriate words from ever being voiced.

It was painful to make these discoveries about myself. Much of my humor and haste to speak without thinking was the result of my own insecurity, desire to be recognized, and false need to assume responsibility for the happiness of others.

What I truly needed were major changes in both the ways I *spoke* and the ways I *thought.* So I started spending time in silence not only to pray, but also to reflect. I started listening for the impact my words made on others. I also started listening for what my words said about me. What did they reflect? What was it that was coming out of my mouth?

As a result of my reflections, I began working at speaking only words that I would feel comfortable with anyone's hearing in any setting, under any circumstances. In other words, I began to try never to speak words that I would want hidden from others. This was easier said than done. I was sickened by my growing awareness of the number of careless words that I spoke which were duplicitous at best and destructive at worst. James, in his Epistle, writes, "a forest is set ablaze by a small fire! And the tongue is a fire!" I discovered this to be completely true of me. His words are uncompromising: "Anyone who makes no mistakes in speaking is perfect, able to keep the whole body in check with a bridle." I wanted to learn to keep my words in check. It would take time — lots of it.

But I thought back to Abraham, and I realized that it took him a lot of time as well. Abraham was seventy-five years old when he departed for Canaan. It wasn't till he was almost one hundred that he became the father of Isaac (when Sarah was ninety). During the intervening years, Abraham had to do much soul-work. But he had great help from God. In spite of Abraham's struggles, God still loved him. God still spoke to him. Abraham continued to listen to God as best he could. And his ability to recognize the Voice and to respond grew in strength.

Abraham's story provided not only the challenge, but also the hope and encouragement that I needed. At first, keeping my mouth and my humor in check required vigilance and enormous effort. When I blew it, I was terribly upset with myself. But then I would reflect on the words of Brother Lawrence, the seventeenth-century monk. He teaches us not to beat up on ourselves. He recommends that, instead, we confess our shortcomings to God simply and clearly, trusting that God will give us the grace to make the improvements we need to make.

I tried to remember these words. And over time God strengthened my desire to speak constructive words with greater and greater love until it became habit.

# A Hard Heart

*I have observed the misery of my people who are in Egypt; I have heard their cry on account of their taskmasters. Indeed, I know their sufferings, and I have come down to deliver them from the Egyptians, and to bring them up out of that land to a good and broad land, a land flowing with milk and honey.*

— God, in Exodus 3:7–8, NRSV

PHARAOH'S HEART WAS HARD. I sit in my study pondering this statement. It seems like a curious way to put things. What does it mean to say that someone's heart is hard?

We use the phrase "a heart of stone." What does this mean?

If one's heart is stone, does this mean that nothing can penetrate it? Does everything bounce off? Would a heart of stone feel nothing — have no compassion, no empathy, or no love? Is a heart of stone a heart incapable of taking in someone else's hurt, pain, fear, hunger, hopes, desires, dreams, despair, or sorrow?

It seemed to me that a person with a hard heart would be doomed to live in isolation — cut off from others. Feeling no compassion, the hard of heart would also feel no joy. Unwilling to feel another's pain, the hard of heart would feel no love, no peace.

Why is that?

Pharaoh's story is quite simple. He knew nothing about the Israelites. And that is because he knew few, if any, Israelites.

51

The Israelites had once been important help to Egypt in a time of famine. An Israelite named Joseph had become prime minister for an earlier Pharaoh. And because Joseph was attentive to God's words, messages, and directions, and because Joseph was a man of uncommon integrity and strength of character, he was able to save both the Egyptians and his own family, who had rejected him, from starvation.

For reasons that the writers of Exodus do not explain, the current Pharaoh knew nothing about this Joseph. We don't know if he was indifferent to history. But we do know that he was ignorant about that key time in his own nation's history. We also know the result. This Pharaoh was indifferent to the Israelites living in his land. He was indifferent to their dignity and humanity. He did not know them as people. And he cared nothing about their hopes and dreams.

Because he was so indifferent, he was willing to enslave them. This Pharaoh set taskmasters over the Israelites. The taskmasters treated the slaves harshly. Their forced labor was backbreaking and debilitating. Pharaoh's treatment of the Israelites was completely ruthless. His cruelty was thoroughly premeditated. Their suffering could not have been more miserable.

Pharaoh also attempted to limit the reproduction of the Israelites. He ordered the Egyptian women who served as midwives to the Hebrews to kill every male born to a Hebrew slave. But because the grace of God was upon these Hebrews, most of the children were delivered safely — both from their mothers at birth and from Pharaoh's solution to the problem that he imagined the Hebrews posed. They escaped infanticide.

One of those baby boys who was safely delivered was placed by his mother in a basket, which she fashioned of reeds and smeared with pitch so it would be waterproof. She placed the basket harboring the baby in the Nile. The basket served as an ark in which the baby was saved, just as Noah and his family were saved from the Flood hundreds of years earlier. It was Pharaoh's daughter who discovered the basket and baby. When word got out, it was through the vigilant intercession of the baby's sister that the child was returned to his mother to be nursed. After the child grew, his mother returned him to Pharaoh's daughter, who named him Moses, which means "drawn out of water."

Even as Moses grew into adulthood, Pharaoh's heart grew ever more hard, and his cruelty and ruthlessness increased. Because the Israelites were so miserable, they cried to God. God heard their cry. And God answered.

God made his answer to Moses, who was tending the flock of his father-in-law, Jethro. Moses noticed a bush. The bush was on fire. It was burning and yet, miraculously, was not consumed. Filled with curiosity and wonder, Moses turned to observe this marvel. He stopped what he was doing and gave the burning bush his full, undivided attention.

Out of the fire, Moses heard the Voice of God. The Voice spoke to Moses, addressing him directly. The Voice commanded Moses to remove his shoes, for he was standing on holy ground in the presence of the Most Holy God. The Voice identified himself as the God of Abraham, Isaac, and Jacob. God then spoke of the Israelite slaves. God's words expressed a heart aflame with compassion for suffering: "I have observed the misery of my people who are in Egypt; I have heard their cry on account of their taskmasters. Indeed, I know their sufferings, and I have come down to deliver them from the Egyptians, and to bring them up out of that land to a good and broad land, a land flowing with milk and honey." God gave heed to the people who were oppressed, in pain, suffering the harsh agony of heartless cruelty.

And this God had a calling for Moses — to be the prophet and instrument who would assist God in bringing his compassion to fulfillment and completion by delivering the Israelites from slavery and oppression. God commanded Moses to appear before Pharaoh and demand the release of God's people.

In the Old Testament, a person of Sloth has a heart of stone — a heartless indifference and unruly apathy that poisons one's every motive and design.

Moses obeyed. But he encountered a formidable obstacle — a merciless Pharaoh. Day after day, Pharaoh's heart had grown ever more hard. He had made himself increasingly indifferent to the pain and suffering of the Israelites, which he himself had caused. And the consequence was that when Moses appeared before him with a message from God, Pharaoh was obstinate in his indifference. His apathy had become headstrong. The writers of Exodus don't use the word "Sloth." That word would come hundreds of years later. But when "Sloth" came into usage, it meant the same as a "hard heart." In the Old Testament, a person of Sloth has a heart of stone — a heartless indifference and unruly apathy that poisons one's every motive and design. Sloth is the hard heart of militant indifference that leads us to refuse God. And the writers of Exodus have rendered a Slothful, hard heart all the easier to recognize by setting Pharaoh's hard heart in sharp contrast with the ever mindful compassion of God.

What happens when a heart is too hopelessly hard? During the last two thousand years many a thoughtful Christian writer has suggested that the penalty for sin is more sin. Sin begets sin. St. Paul had this in mind when he said that we reap what we sow. We see this same idea in the story of Pharaoh's hard heart. God saw to it that Pharaoh reaped what he sowed. Because Pharaoh was so militant in his indifference, God made his heart all the more hard. The penalty for hardness of heart was ever greater indifference. Pharaoh was not only uninterested in the humanity, dignity, pain, and suffering of others, he was apathetic toward God. God called upon Moses to perform ten wonders. Moses was to initiate ten plagues, each of which would call Pharaoh's attention to what God was planning to do for the Israelites in Egypt. But Pharaoh was indifferent to the suffering of the Israelites, and, unlike Moses, he was adamant in his refusal to recognize God and his wonders. This meant that Pharaoh's hard heart finally rendered him blind to what God was accomplishing all around Pharaoh and before his very eyes. The story conveys this most clearly in the ninth plague that Pharaoh had to suffer — darkness. The darkness was absolute. In the dark everyone was completely cut off from the Presence of God, whose first words were, "Let there be light." Pharaoh was not only unmoved by this God of light; he had no care for life itself. He therefore reaped the ultimate plague — death of the firstborn of all living for whom he bore responsibility. For better or for worse, Pharaoh reaped plagues sown of Sloth.

At this same time the Israelites were reaping the fruits of their cries to God. In response to their prayers, God made it his purpose to rescue the Israelites from slavery in Egypt and to bring them to a good land flowing with milk and honey. Having issued the plagues, God rescued the Israelites by leading them out of Egypt, guiding them as a pillar of cloud by day and as a pillar of fire by night. At this point the story takes an important turn. The writers of Exodus are quick to show us that Sloth is not a problem that is limited to or associated with one particular nation or ethnic group. The Israelites are also vulnerable to a spell of Sloth. Theirs is the indifference of forgetfulness. Although thrilled to be escaping Egypt, their joy was short-lived. No sooner did they come up against the waters of the Red Sea, but they looked back and saw the Egyptians in hot pursuit. In spite of the fact that it is God who was leading them, their reaction was to give Moses the first of many a scolding that he would be forced to endure: "Was it because there were no graves in Egypt that you have taken us away to die in the wilderness? What have you done to us, bringing us out of Egypt?" How soon we forget.

I am not suggesting that all forgetfulness is an expression of Sloth. But in this case, it was. The Israelites not only ignored God's immediate Presence but also ignored all that God had done to bring them to that point. They conveniently ignored all that God had done for them and the trust and loyalty that God's Presence merits. And yet, in spite of their apathy and forgetful faithlessness, God still parted the Red Sea, allowing a people who hastened to distrust him to cross safely on a dry riverbed. Finally, God drowned Egyptian horses and riders in the sea. Israel's deliverance from slavery to safety was complete.

But the Israelites did not nourish the memory of what God had done for them. Their forgetfulness seemed to have a will of its own. Their complaining was chronic. And they conspired to rebel against God, Moses, and Aaron. The consequence was that there were many times when God was fed up with the people. And God let Moses know about it. "How long will these people despise me? And how long will they refuse to believe in me, in spite of all the signs that I have done among them? I will strike them with pestilence and disinherit them, and I will make of you a nation greater and mightier than they." The problem was that the people had become apathetic. *Either willfully or by neglect, they had forgotten the goodness of God. They had ignored the kindness that God had faithfully shown them, time and again.* Instead, they all too easily fell away from the truth that God's purpose was to make them into a New Creation. This required wisdom and forethought on the part of God and patient perseverance on the part of the people. The people, however, unconsciously slid into that debilitating inertia of indifference. They hastened to the vulgar slumber of apathy and became possessed by Sloth. They became indifferent to God at the very moment when God helped them out of their trouble. And the symptom of their Sloth was joyless amnesia. Their forgetfulness was a symptom of careless mindlessness.

Here I sit, pondering such hardness of heart. I read in my Bible of a king who was unmoved by the pain that others suffered or by the wonders of God. I read of a king who was indifferent to the dignity and humanity of a fellow human being. And I read of a people who became willfully forgetful of God even as God was fully present and offering them loving help. Wonders were all about them. The people were in the midst of these wonders. And yet they were blind. They could not — rather, they would not — see God in those wonders. And I wonder how many wonders I am missing every day. How soon do I forget God? And whose pain and suffering do I conveniently ignore?

# A Lukewarm Reception

*I know your works. You are neither cold nor hot.*

— Jesus, in Revelation 3:15, NRSV

I SAT WITH A COLLEAGUE in a restaurant. He had recently left a pastorate at a church where he was never truly welcome. The reason was simple. His predecessor was beloved, and the congregation couldn't — or wouldn't — let his memory go. They didn't want to lose their previous pastor. And the fact that their previous pastor was ready to move on was lost on them. They were grieving. That is perfectly understandable. But the consequence was that they gave the new pastor a reception that might best be described as lukewarm.

It went like this on the new pastor's first Sunday. The Lay Leader welcomed him by saying to the new pastor and his wife, "There's a corsage for you in the refrigerator in the kitchen. If you want it, you can put it on." That was it. That was the extent of the reception for the new pastor and his wife.

This tepid reception might also be described as Slothful. Whether or not the Lay Leader felt indifferent, he certainly expressed indifference to the new pastor and his wife. We pastors are aware that when we go to a new church, our congregation will be grieving the departure of our predecessor. And as best we can, we will honor the grieving process of our new flock. I can remember my first Sunday at a new church. I followed a pastor who had been there a long time, and I worked especially hard on preparing my first sermon. So when I walked into the sanctuary on my first Sunday and a man greeted me, asking, "Are you nervous?" I said, "No, but I'm feeling excited about being here." He said, "Well, we are!" I laughed. It was a wonderful moment in which we connected. And in our brief exchange, we both acknowledged both our grief and our hope. What was joyful for me was that Nancy's and my reception was anything but lukewarm. Grieving as they were, our new congregation was deliberately caring.

When I read the New Testament and pay attention to the various receptions that Jesus received, I am rather stunned by the number of receptions that were lukewarm. In the seventh chapter of Luke, Jesus has been invited to the home of Simon the Pharisee. There were certain customs that a host would offer the guest that said to the guest, "You are welcome here." First, the host would greet the guest with the kiss of peace. This is not unlike our shaking hands, or perhaps like greeting our guest with a kind hug. The host's servants would then come in and wash the guest's feet. If the host was too poor to afford servants, the host would perform the foot-washing himself. Finally, the guest would be anointed with oil. When Jesus entered the home of Simon, Simon offered none of these common courtesies to Jesus. Simon instead expressed apathy. The reception he offered Jesus was lukewarm at best. Chilly would better describe Simon's behavior. Simon was indifferent to the humanity and dignity of Jesus. This is Sloth — a lukewarm apathy for a fellow human being or for something that matters greatly.

The book of Revelation also offers a portrayal of Jesus' receiving a lukewarm reception. The focus is on the behavior of the people of the church of Laodicea. The church of Laodicea had a wealthy congregation. They were not struggling with the poverty that threatened so many of the early Christian congregations. This congregation enjoyed material resources and purchasing power in abundance. In the economic sense, they had it made.

As the writer of Revelation turned to this congregation, we discover that they were in the middle of a celebration of Holy Communion. The problem is that they had neglected to invite Jesus. While the congregation was on the inside, celebrating the Lord's Supper, Jesus was on the outside, calling: "Listen, I am standing at the door knocking; if you hear my voice and open the door, I will come in to you and eat with you and you with me." This congregation was indifferent to Jesus. Their reception for Jesus was lukewarm, and that is because their faith was lukewarm. It was neither hot nor cold. Their faith was instead rather neutral. This congregation was more or less apathetic, indifferent, and careless. This is what the New Testament means by Sloth — a relationship to Jesus of neglect and apathy.

I can still remember when this awareness of a lukewarm reception for Jesus first came to me. I was reading the story of Jesus' crucifixion, with all that led up to it. I think that the first aspect of Sloth was when Jesus was with his disciples in the Garden of Gethsemane. Jesus went there to pray. He was distressed, agitated, and filled with agony. He was about to be arrested, taken by force, tried, and crucified. His arrest was a betrayal. Judas was handing Jesus over to the Romans for money. Jesus had been teaching his disciples that his death was completely necessary. But like so many who want to follow Jesus, these disciples were having great trouble grasping or accepting the necessity of his death. Jesus had reviewed with them the reasons for his death several times. Still, they had great difficulty understanding. And the idea of his willing acceptance of his own death petrified them.

Even though Jesus believed in the complete importance of what he was planning, and even though he went to his death voluntarily, his actual *following through* was anything but easy. It is one thing to say, "This is my calling; this is what I plan to do." It is quite another to fulfill the calling — to bring it to fruition. It was about this challenge of actually following through — in full awareness that the pain, suffering, and agony would be unbearable — that Jesus came to the garden to pray.

This congregation was more or less apathetic, indifferent, and careless. This is what the New Testament means by Sloth — a relationship to Jesus of neglect and apathy.

When I first studied this passage in earnest, one element above all others haunted me. It had to do with the response and behavior of Jesus' disciples. The directions that Jesus gave to Peter, James, and John were unambiguous, simple, and clear. "Sit here while I pray. Don't fall asleep. Watch." Jesus asked for their attention. He asked that their attention be undivided. He wanted them alert and focused. Yet, in spite of the simplicity of Jesus' request, Peter, James, and John fell asleep. They slept through the entire episode. "Their eyes were very heavy."

When Jesus questioned their inability, or unwillingness, to stay awake, the disciples were virtually paralyzed. They were unable to answer Jesus. It was as though they were struggling to wake from a drunken stupor.

The occasion called for the disciples to exercise sustained, vigilant concentration. The situation merited their undivided attention. But they slept — through one of the most momentous times in history.

I was beginning to realize that what I read on the page represented more than mere laziness. I was seeing a kind of sleeping *sickness*. The attitude of Jesus' disciples was cavalier, casual, and careless. They failed to discern what the circumstances called for. And this was in part because they were ignoring what the situation called for. *Their impulse to sluggishness was driven by their indifference to Jesus' calling — to his vocation.* Lukewarm about what Jesus was trying to teach them, they gave little thought to perseverance, to staying *with* Jesus.

It was in studying this passage that it hit me: The disciples labored under the weight of Sloth. They were debilitated by an inertia that included laziness, but far more. What we see in the Garden of Gethsemane is laziness, ignorance, apathy, indifference, carelessness, and inertia — all feeding each other, all in connivance. And this Sloth works itself out in the disciples' closing their eyes to Jesus, to his trials and challenges, to the matters he is trying to teach, and to the results that he is struggling to accomplish. This is Sloth — a lukewarmness bred of sheer carelessness for God's extraordinary purposes, which are seeking to unfold before our open eyes.

# Unreflected Grace

*Should you not have had mercy on your fellow slave, as I had mercy on you?*                    —Matthew 18:33, NRSV

I IMAGINE THAT one of the remarkable reasons Jesus had for telling stories was their power to help us reflect on the genuine. His stories, which in some ways are about the most ordinary of things, ask us to ponder, What makes ordinary life extraordinary? By extraordinary, I don't mean grandiose or self-aggrandizing; I mean *authentic*. I am still finding that the stories that Jesus composed and told for his listeners help us to hear, imagine, reflect, and envision life with continually increased insight and understanding. His stories give us eyes with which to see.

One story, which I have lived with for almost thirty years, is called the Parable of the Unforgiving Servant. As I began to search the Bible to understand Sloth, I wondered whether its subtitle might be Unreflected Grace. In the eighteenth chapter of Matthew, Jesus is speaking of the kingdom of heaven. And he likens it to a king who wished to settle accounts with his servants. As the story opens, the king is just discovering that one servant owes him ten thousand talents. Now "talent" is one of two words in this story that require a little explanation. When Jesus speaks of a talent, he isn't thinking in terms of a natural God-given ability for, say, music, art, or sports. That's our meaning for the term. The talent that Jesus spoke of is a sum of money. One talent equals ten thousand denarii. Now, I realize that I haven't helped a whole lot because the term *denarius* isn't in most people's vocabularies either. But again, the concept is simple. In Jesus' day, a denarius was a *day's wage*. It was probably not unlike our idea of a minimum wage. A denarius was the amount of money a laborer would earn working for one day — probably a twelve-hour shift.

If we do the math, we discover that this servant owed his king one hundred million days' wages (100,000,000 denarii divided by 10,000 = 10,000 talents). This is a huge sum of money. Jesus doesn't tell us how the servant came to owe his master so much. And Jesus doesn't take much time to reflect on the irresponsibility of this servant's stewardship. He simply tells us what the servant owed. And what the servant owed was enormous.

The king's reaction was outrage. Exploding in anger, the king ordered the sale of the servant and his wife and children and that payment be made. Were we again to do the math, we would learn that this wouldn't accomplish much by way of satisfying the debt. The historians have discovered that, what with the going rate for slaves, the sale of an entire family would not total even one talent, let alone ten thousand. What happens, though, is that the servant, in response to the king's command that the servant be sold into slavery, falls before the king and pleads for mercy and patience: "Have patience on me, and I will pay you everything!" The servant isn't thinking about the fact that he would have to work some one hundred million days to pay off the debt. But suddenly, spontaneously, and with no hint that he was going to do this, the king forgives the entire debt. This servant has been let off. Just like that, he is free.

No sooner does this free and forgiven servant leave the presence of the king than he comes upon a fellow servant who owes him one hundred denarii — one millionth of what he himself has just been forgiven. What does this first servant do? He seizes his fellow servant by the throat, demanding immediate payment. The fellow servant falls to his knees and pleads, "Have patience with me, and I will pay you everything!" These are the precise words with which the first servant supplicated the king. The only difference in their situations is that it would be possible, eventually, for the second servant to repay the first. The first servant, on the other hand, would never have had sufficient time to make amends.

Then suddenly the answer was there. Jesus' story reflected the answer from the page in my Bible. The unforgiving servant was completely unreflective. He was offered grace, but he didn't receive it.

The response of the first servant is as different from the way in which the king responded to him as light is different from darkness. Instead of forgiving the debt, or at least granting the requested time, the first servant orders the imprisonment of his fellow servant *until the debt is paid.*

Other responses to this ruthless behavior quickly follow. Fellow servants observe what is happening. They are aware of the similarity between the two servants' situations. And they are aware that the first servant, who is acting so mercilessly, has just received more forgiveness than he asked for and could reasonably have expected. These observing servants are deeply disturbed — so much so that they report the behavior of the forgiven servant to their king.

The king is once again outraged. But this time his anger reflects the injustice that the forgiven servant is perpetrating. The king summons the servant whom he has forgiven into his presence and says with utter condemnation, "You wicked servant! I forgave you all that debt. Could you not have had mercy on your fellow servant, as I had mercy on you?" And in his anger, the king delivers the first servant to the jailers until he should pay his entire debt. The king incarcerates the first servant for life.

I had known for years that the forgiven servant had failed somehow to internalize the grace he received. I had recognized that for the grace to become complete, it had to take root in the forgiven servant so he in turn could offer the same grace to someone else. What I did not recognize for many years was the reason for this. So I began to ask why. What is Jesus showing us? What is he portraying, right before our eyes? What is there for any and all to see?

And then suddenly the answer was there. Jesus' story reflected the answer from the page in my Bible. The unforgiving servant was completely unreflective. He was offered grace, but he didn't receive it. I started looking for evidence of the servant's pondering the grace he was offered, and I couldn't find it because it wasn't there. The servant didn't think about this grace in relationship to himself, his circumstances, or his character. Consequently, when faced with someone who was similarly indebted to him, he saw no analogy between their situations, and he could not reflect this same grace back to the one who owed him. The grace wasn't reflected back to his debtor because it had never penetrated his own consciousness. Why was that? What does Jesus give us to observe?

Was not this unforgiving servant stubbornly indifferent? Was he not indifferent to the pity and compassion that had been offered to him? Was he not indifferent to the similarity of the debt he was owed with the debt from which he had been released? Was he not indifferent to the benefits of grace both received and offered? Was he not indifferent to the consequences of the unwillingness to forgive? Was he not indifferent to the huge difference in degree between what he was owed and what he himself had owed? And was he not indifferent to the inappropriateness of his own reaction, which was out of proportion with the offense he suffered?

What I finally saw behind Jesus' penetrating story was the Sloth that had thoroughly poisoned the unforgiving servant. He was under a spell of obstinate apathy that made him unwilling to reflect the compassion and grace he himself had received. I now observed a servant who was unwilling to reflect on the grace in his own life, situation, and character. And I saw someone who, because of Sloth, was unwilling to reflect the grace he had received to a fellow traveler in this life.

From these musings, a new understanding was beginning to emerge for me. Doesn't a willingness to reflect on the benefits of grace strengthen our humanity while it also deepens our relationships? And without that, doesn't Sloth attack us right at the core of our human dignity?

# TRAINED EMOTIONS

*Without the aid of trained emotions the intellect is powerless against the animal organism.*

— C. S. Lewis, *The Abolition of Man*

I WAS TRYING to help the CEO of the Community Food Bank in Tucson raise funds to increase their storage space for food. His name is Punch Woods. I was his pastor at the time, and he became a wonderful friend. I learned more about hunger from Punch than from just about anybody else. The community that Punch and I both served had a hundred thousand citizens who missed eight or more meals a month, sixty-five thousand of whom were children. There were days when that staggering number was more than I could wrap my mind around.

One day Punch and I were meeting to do some planning. He told me about something that had happened just two days earlier in a small United Methodist Church in the Tucson area. A Community Food Bank staff member was meeting with a committee at the church in an effort to solicit their support for the fund-raising effort. A woman who was a member of the committee suddenly made an urgent plea for support from all who were present.

The woman told the group that she was a cafeteria worker at an elementary school that served federally funded breakfasts and lunches to many of the students. On Monday of that week, she had arrived at the cafeteria at 5:00 a.m. to prepare breakfast. When she arrived, two boys on their bicycles were waiting for her.

Surprised by their presence, the woman had asked, "What are you two boys doing here so early? You know I don't start serving till 6:30."

The boys had replied, "We know. But we haven't eaten since Friday."

That was all that the cafeteria worker needed to say to persuade the people in her church to support the Food Bank's efforts.

This woman's story stunned me. For some reason, my mind — and my heart, for that matter — couldn't help but grasp the story of these two boys. I remembered that Punch had told me about the many children who regularly miss meals. One of the things that hit me with these two boys was that they had missed seven meals in a row — dinner on Friday, three meals on Saturday, and three on Sunday.

It wasn't till years later, reading a book by C. S. Lewis, that I came to understand something about what the hunger of those two boys meant to me.

C. S. Lewis (1898–1963) was a fellow in English language and literature at Magdalen College, Oxford University. He was also one of the most influential Christian writers of the twentieth century and the best-selling Christian author of all time. One of his remarkable volumes is entitled *The Abolition of Man*. In this book, Lewis addressed the *feelings* and *affections* we have for others. His remarks are somewhat similar to the thinking of St. Augustine, who argued that there is such a thing as loving the right things and loving them in the right way. St. Augustine referred to this as "the order of loves." In the same vein, C. S. Lewis argues that there are affections that are right, and there are affections that are wrong. And the rightness or wrongness comes not from how we happen to be feeling at a particular time, but from the *object* of our affections and the *situation* that a person is in. Sentiments are right and just to the degree that they are appropriate to a person's humanity and situation. Unjust sentiments fail to grasp and reflect the situation that is confronting us. These attitudes *ignore* what the dignity of the people and their circumstances merit. This kind of militant ignorance is Sloth. Sloth is indifference and apathy to people and situations that merit love and justice.

When I reflected on Lewis's words, I realized that I had been accustomed to thinking of feelings as neither right nor wrong. The Christian culture in which I had grown up said that feelings just are. Lewis startled me because he suggested something completely different. I recognized that those two boys, who had missed seven meals in a row over a span of three days, *merited* my love and compassion. When we hear their story, tears come to our eyes. Lewis showed us that the tears come because the two boys are precious children of God. They have a dignity that is absolute: their worth is infinite; it cannot be modified. We know this, and we know it absolutely.

To ignore their dignity, to be indifferent to it, is to be Slothful. Among other things, Sloth means a willful failure to love the right things in the right way. And one of the reasons for this failure is a failure to develop the feelings and affections — in a word, *sentiments* — that are right and proper. We have seen these unjust sentiments in an extreme and terrible situation: a Nazi concentration camp. Some of the soldiers are playing a game. They are throwing live babies into the air and spearing them on their bayonets. As they do so, the soldiers are laughing. And as they engage in casual conversation, they ignore the fact that some of the babies that they are carrying on their bayonets are still alive.

What's our response to such a situation going to be? Is this not one of the most horrifying behaviors imaginable? Is this not more than we can fathom? Such atrocities fill us with shock and outrage. And well they should. This kind of cruel behavior merits nothing short of condemnation. And the merit is absolute. Their laughter at the unspeakable atrocities that they themselves are executing is categorically diabolical and completely damnable.

What Lewis saw is that such behavior is the fruit of sentiments that are totally perverted and absolutely wrong. And he used the word "sentiments" because he wanted to emphasize that the feelings we have for and responses we have to others are to a significant degree *conditioned*. Personal sentiments are never only subjective and idiosyncratic. We have to be *taught* these sentiments. Sentiments — feelings and affections — are a part of our nature, to be sure. But human nature is incomplete. Only through nurture — education and learning — do we become a more complete human being. And becoming complete includes the cultivation — the training and conditioning — of our sentiments.

This education includes training the heart in the order of loves. A person has to learn to recognize what merits humility, reverence, awe, respect, veneration, and the like. Lewis writes, "The little human animal will not at first have the right responses. It must be trained to feel pleasure, liking, disgust, and hatred at those things which really are pleasant, likeable, disgusting, and hateful." Suppose, for example, that a child in his or her early years frequently witnesses Mother or Father expressing contempt for other people and perhaps for each other. And suppose further that the response of the parents to the child is one of frequent indifference. The child may even witness violence in the home. Perhaps Dad beats Mom. Perhaps

71

Dad expresses apathy for Mom's legitimate needs and her humanity. And let us further assume that the child, naturally holding his or her parents in high esteem, has little, if any, intellectual defense against acquiring a view of the world that is largely conditioned by indifference. What happens is that the child's sentiments are conditioned by joyless apathy and contempt. The child fails to acquire *just* sentiments. Such a failure is devastating. Lewis writes, "For every one pupil who needs to be guarded from a weak excess of sensibility, there are three who need to be awakened from the slumber of cold vulgarity." Does this not sound like those Nazi soldiers? Do not their actions stem from a complete perversion of sentiments — a willful indifference and militant apathy toward human dignity, the preciousness of life, our connection to each other, and reverence for God?

Unjust sentiments fail to grasp and reflect the situation that is confronting us. These attitudes *ignore* what the dignity of the people and their circumstances merit. This kind of militant ignorance is Sloth. Sloth is indifference and apathy to people and situations that merit love and justice.

C. S. Lewis recognized that our minds are in large part rational. But mere reason is never enough. It is one thing to know the numbers. I may memorize a number that says there are sixty-five thousand children in my community who are hungry much of the time. And such reasoned knowledge is important. But if I know that two boys on their bicycles in front of the cafeteria at 5:00 a.m. have not eaten for days, and my heart fails to feel the deep compassion, I may not be moved to love them and offer my help. What Lewis recognized is that "without the aid of trained emotions the intellect is powerless against the animal organism." Without training our feelings, we run the risk of becoming apathetic and indifferent — in a word, Slothful. Lewis put it this way: "The head rules the belly through the chest — the seat . . . of emotions organized by trained habit into stable sentiments. The Chest — Magnanimity — Sentiment — these are the indispensable liaison officers between cerebral man and visceral man. It may even be said that it is by this middle element that man is man: for by his intellect he is mere spirit and by his appetite mere animal."

I spent many days pondering the plight of those two boys. I felt a nudge that I could not ignore to compose something that would convey not only the hunger of the boys, but what it means for us to recognize their humanity as well as their hunger. How might we come to recognize our own occasions to be Slothful — our own periods of indifference and apathy? And just as important, how might we reflect on our experiences and respond with such great love that the hungry are fed and we are transformed? This is the story I composed:

*Miss Smith took the greatest pride in her teaching. She had earned a reputation for being severely demanding, and it was a reputation in which she took a mighty pride. Miss Smith maintained her reputation with an ever-present intimidating scowl. Her demeanor expressed the single-minded ferocity with which she drilled knowledge into the heads of her students. Moreover, Miss Smith bore no tolerance for the lazy student. She despised unpreparedness. Education was a privilege to be seized upon with uncompromised devotion.*

*In this particular school year, there was one boy in her class who drove her to seethe. He was never prepared. When she called on him, he never knew the answer. His concentration was in the toilet. His laziness was appalling. He was even in the unforgivable habit of falling asleep while she taught. To add insult to her already tarnished ego, he sat in the front row. And were that not enough, no measure of discipline that she could devise produced any result. And no teacher was a more practiced disciplinarian than she.*

*The entire faculty knew about the lad. Miss Smith saw to it. Rarely did a lunch session in the teacher's lounge pass without her customary tirade and lamentation over the student's clearly spoiled behavior.*

*Then one day, everything was different. As Miss Smith stood before the class and taught, this boy, sitting right there in front of her, was completely alert. Miss Smith would ask a question. He would raise his hand. Miss Smith would call on him. He would give an answer. The answer was correct. Miss Smith was astonished. It completely spoiled her day. At lunchtime, she had nothing to complain about. "I wonder what's eating at Miss Smith?" her colleagues whispered.*

*After lunch, Miss Smith returned to her room for the afternoon round of teaching. For the most part, the results were the same. Miss Smith didn't know what to think — until three o'clock came.*

*The bell rang, announcing the end of the school day. As was her custom, having made sure that each student remembered his or her coat and books, Miss Smith returned to her desk. There she espied a brown paper bag, inside of which were two cans of food and a note. Miss Smith read:*

Dear Miss Smith,

   We don't have much food at our house. Most of the time, I'm really hungry. I never get to eat breakfast before school.

But Miss Smith, this week my mom went to a food bank! They gave us lots of good food.

It's really hard to stay awake when you're hungry. And you feel really grumpy.

Miss Smith, I've noticed that like me, you are really grumpy sometimes. And I was wondering if you don't get enough to eat either. So I asked my mom if I could give you some of the food from our stash. I'm sorry it isn't more, but I hope it helps.

*The boy's words hit Miss Smith right in the chest. It was as if Miss Smith saw herself for the first time. She recognized her own heartlessness. She not only saw what she was doing to the boy, she saw what she was doing to her class. She had become so indifferent to what really mattered that she was inadvertently teaching her own students to be thoughtless, to be callous and unfeeling. Feelings of guilt and shame completely overwhelmed her. "How could I have been so callous? How could I have failed to know?"*

*Miss Smith knew what she had to do. She made confession and appropriate apologies to her fellow faculty members. And on the next day, she instructed the lad to arrive at school one half hour early — each and every morning. But the purpose would not be additional instruction. This was an invitation to break bread. Every day Miss Smith would serve the two of them breakfast — right there at her desk. And over the course of what would become a remarkable school year, the boy's forgiveness and love would become the gift that changed Miss Smith from heartless indifference to awareness and generosity nourished by the gift of the boy's gracious life.*

# SLOTH AT ITS DEADLIEST

*For every one pupil who needs to be guarded from a weak excess of sensibility, there are three who need to be awakened from the slumber of cold vulgarity.*

—C. S. Lewis, *The Abolition of Man*

I T WAS A TUESDAY. The date was April 20, 1999. Would that it were burned into our collective consciousness like September 11, 2001. For the people of Littleton, Colorado, it no doubt is. That is the day that Eric Harris, age eighteen, and Dylan Klebold, age seventeen, unleashed heartless cruelty on their community, which shocked and sickened decent people everywhere. Those two youths burst into the library of Columbine High School and announced their intent to blow up the school and murder fellow students. Harris and Klebold shouted, "Today is your day to die!" As they shot and killed fellow students, they were laughing, commenting on how much fun they were having terrorizing fellow human beings. Michael Moore produced a film entitled *Bowling for Columbine.* (It seems that on the morning of April 20, 1999, prior to committing their crimes and suicides, Harris and Klebold had gone bowling.) With the theater audience, I sat and watched in horror as Moore showed security camera footage of the carnage at the high school. I cannot remember witnessing anything more chilling.

With countless others I have read many an article about Columbine High in an effort to sort things out in my mind. I wanted to come to an adequate understanding of what happened. I was curious to know what went wrong. One writer whom I admire is Wendy Zoba, an editor for *Christianity Today*. One of the things I like about her coverage of the event is that she set her sights on what she calls "something bigger." She points out that this event "has been dissected into many parts: gun-control issues; uncensored access to dangerous information on the Internet; the violent media culture; the cliquish school culture; the need for parental oversight; the separation of church and state." All of these are important issues, and none can be ignored in the search for a comprehensive understanding of Harris's and Klebold's actions. What made Zoba's study remarkable was her sense that there was a *meta-variable* that touched each of the other important factors that came into play in this sickening episode. A meta-variable is a single factor that touches and influences all of the other factors, in this case leading Harris and Klebold to act as they did. To get a handle on what a meta-variable is, think of the seasoning we put on food. Salt, for example, affects the entire eating experience. It flavors the food. Similarly, when I drink, say, tea, I might drink it plain, or I might add cream or sugar or both. But instead of cream and sugar, imagine putting arsenic in someone's drink. Simply put, the food is now laced with poison. A meta-variable is like that. It consists of some one thing that touches, shapes, and deeply affects all related variables of significance.

Wendy Zoba had a hunch that there was something at large in the Columbine episode that affected everything like poison. And her goal was to identify this variable. So how did she go about doing her work? How did she set out to find this *something bigger?*

She first examined the experiences of those who were involved — those who were present in that high school on that horrible day. Zoba picked up on a particular inkling, or intuition, that various parents, students, teachers, and pastors reported time and again. The inkling had two parts. The first was an unmistakable awareness that *the Lord was with us* through the entire ordeal. The people were able to identify God's Presence. The Presence was both clear and undeniable. When the people of Littleton shared this awareness with each other, they all understood each other. The second part of the inkling consisted of recognizing that what Harris and Klebold perpetrated was sheer evil. People knew that evil was confronting them directly. Moreover, this was a recognition that they shared. It was something upon which they were in agreement. And they possessed the wherewithal to call it evil and to avoid reducing it to some sort of psychological or value-neutral term. Having been confronted by evil made its naming inescapable. Zoba reports that as the killing unfolded, the students knew themselves to be "at the epicenter of evil, totally disconnected from their community, their families, the Author of all that is good."

This insight led Zoba to want to learn something about the nature of the evil that confronted the people of Littleton. In order to understand this critical issue, Zoba focused on Harris's and Klebold's behavior as they perpetrated their atrocities. What caught Zoba's attention was the sheer pleasure that Harris and Klebold received from their actions. They laughed at the people they murdered. They taunted them even as they killed them. They ridiculed and humiliated their fellow students as they watched them die. These actions were utterly heinous. They attacked the core of the dignity of our common humanity. That two young men should find the premeditated murder of fellow high school students to be pleasurable and even laughable is as wrong as wrong can be.

Young Lance Kirkland lay on the ground, crying, "Help me." Dylan Klebold approached him and responded, "Sure, I'll help you," and then shot Kirkland in the face.

Rachel Scott lay on the floor, crying. The reports concerning what happened to her are not all in agreement, but Scott's friends told her family that the killers confronted her with a question: "Do you believe in God?" Her answer was yes. They immediately put a gun to her temple and killed her.

One of the killers spotted a young man named Isaiah Shoels and said, "Hey look, there's that little nigger." They then shot Shoels three times.

The killers walked up to Cassie Bernall and asked, "Do you believe in God?" She answered yes. The killers then asked, "Why?" They immediately shot her.

The same thing happened to Val Schnurr. The killers approached her. They were shooting. She was crying, "Oh my God, oh my God." They asked her, "Do you believe in God?" Like Cassie Bernall, Val Schnurr said yes. They asked her why, and they immediately shot her as well.

How do we make sense out of this bald-faced evil that so chills and sickens us? What happened here? What is there for us to understand? To her credit, Wendy Zoba found help from C. S. Lewis. She turned to his volume *The Abolition of Man.* In Lewis's terms, they were two young "Men without Chests." Their sentiments — their feelings and affections — were polluted. They were completely unjust; their hearts had atrophied beyond human recognition. *These boys were poisoned by Sloth.* Their apathy was hopelessly militant. Their indifference, sickening. Their laughter was void of any joy. When Harris and Klebold looked at a student, they did not recognize a fellow human being whose dignity, being absolute and established by God, merited the deepest respect. They did not see that though their fellow students were flawed, these flaws did not abolish or extinguish the merit of their dignity. Harris and Klebold did not recognize the preciousness of their fellow students because they were overwhelmingly under the spell of Sloth. This is the meta-variable that Wendy Zoba sensed from the beginning. She knew it was there. She knew that it touched all the other factors with its diabolical poison. Sloth had produced sentiments of sheer heartlessness that created the conditions in which violence in collusion with contempt could unfold in a high school in middle America.

It was in the early Middle Ages that monks began to reflect seriously on the sin of Sloth. When they began to ponder Sloth, they recognized that Sloth is deadly. And as their thinking developed, they included it as one of the Seven Deadly Sins. The Sloth that we saw in Littleton shockingly illustrates why the monks deemed Sloth to be deadly. Harris and Klebold had made themselves indifferent to the preciousness and dignity of a fellow human being. Their indifference and apathy created the internal conditions that made it possible for them to kill in cold blood. In two young men, Harris and Klebold, sadly we witnessed sin at its deadliest.

The term "Deadly" Sin simply means *capital* sin — a sin that leads to other sins. Deadly Sins give birth to other sins. In the case of Harris and Klebold, the Deadly Sin of Sloth gave birth to murder.

Sloth is the *something bigger* that Wendy Zoba sought and found at Columbine. Sloth poisoned everything.

# PARTIAL TRUTH
# IS NOT ENOUGH

*I have given you as a covenant to the people,*
*a light to the nations,*
*to open the eyes that are blind,*
*to bring out the prisoners from the dungeon,*
*from the prison those who sit in darkness.*

—Isaiah 42:6–7, NRSV

W HAT HAPPENS when Sloth gets a hold on our thought processes? Or to put it another way, what happens when our *thought processes* fall under a spell of Sloth? And if Sloth poisons our thinking, how would we notice? The mere ability to recognize Sloth necessitates careful reflection.

As I pondered the breathtaking Wrath that Eric Harris and Dylon Klebold visited on Columbine High School, I found myself thinking how much their actions reminded me of Adolf Hitler. No one has earned greater infamy for calculating cruelty than Adolf Hitler. And if Hitler's indifference and apathy toward the Jews was not absolute, it was certainly as militant as militant can be. Imagine a scenario where we could explore Hitler's thinking. Imagine a situation in which Adolf Hitler offers a defense of the Holocaust that serves as an open window to his thought processes. Novelist George Steiner, who is a distinguished Jewish scholar, has imagined just such a scenario in his stunning novel of 1979, *Portage to San Cristobal of A. H.* The *A. H.* stands for Adolf Hitler. The plot is straightforward: Hitler has not committed suicide in his bunker. He has instead escaped, fleeing to South America. And this has motivated Nazi hunters to search tirelessly for their quarry. By the end of the novel, they have found him. They have Adolf Hitler in custody. Steiner then allows Hitler his day in court. At the climax of the novel, Hitler defends himself.

Hitler begins his defense of the idea of a master race by holding the Jews themselves responsible. He claims that this was *their* idea, and it is an idea that he plundered from them. Hitler's idea of a master race came from their idea of election: the idea that the Jews are a race chosen and set apart for an exclusive covenantal relationship with God. Hitler is even so bold as to suggest that the Jews themselves used the idea of being a chosen race to justify acts of genocide that they themselves perpetrated. The most infamous, says Hitler, is the Battle of Jericho, where the Jews committed wholesale slaughter against the residents of Canaan. Hitler used the same interpretation on the book of Samuel. This book represents the same kind of Jewish genocide against the Philistines. In response to their victory, the people sang in praise of both Saul, who had slain his *thousands*, and David, who had slain his *ten thousands*. It was *because* of this idea of election that the Jews committed genocide, and without it, they would not have. The Jews, claims Hitler, acted as animals — mere brutes.

Some have wondered whether George Steiner hasn't allowed Hitler to vindicate himself. I myself wonder whether he hasn't instead left it up to the reader to identify the flaws in Hitler's hollow argument. They are not difficult to identify. Hitler focuses on the idea of election — being a chosen race, set apart by God. But he conveniently ignores what this chosen race is set apart *for*. Hitler assumes that a covenant of election merely sets a people above the rest of the population. He ignores that the purpose of *this* covenant of election is to constitute a people chosen for the purpose of serving as a light to the nations. God does not choose the Jews for the purpose of lording it over the rest of Earth's people. He calls upon the Jews to live as a community of *servants* for the benefit of others. To this end, God gives these servants heavy responsibility: to show the way to God, to holy living, and to peace.

This isn't the only thing Hitler ignores. He also closes his eyes to the fact that living in *covenant* with God and one another is anything but brute. Living in covenant involves obligations. The obligations are mutual. But this is not to say that the obligations are equal. A covenant is not the same as a contract, pact, or agreement between equals. In covenant, God is superordinate, and the Jews are subordinate. God has obligations to the Jews — to be their faithful God — and the Jews have obligations — faithful obedience to God's commands.

What Hitler does in ignoring the responsibilities and demands that God places upon the Jews is to focus on the Jews' shortcomings throughout their history. The Jews have done many things wrong over the years. They have occasionally been as guilty as any of us in rebelling against God. But what Hitler conveniently ignores is that whereas the Jews have done *some* things wrong, this does not make them *entirely,* or even *primarily*, wrong as a people. Moreover, when they have done wrong, the Jews themselves have held each other accountable for wrongdoing. The Jewish prophets not only do not ignore any wrongdoing of the Jews, they are critical of the Jews when they have done wrong. And this is because accountability is at the heart of living in covenant. The Jews have made some mistakes. But this has never changed what God has *intended* to do through them — to serve the world as a light to the nations.

Why does Hitler willfully ignore all of this? It is because his interpretation of the Jews is conditioned by his studied indifference to the Jews — to their humanity and to their calling. For all his other faults, Steiner's Hitler is under a spell of Sloth. Apathy toward the Jews predominates both his attitudes and his thought processes. Indifference leads him to ignore those parts of the truth that he'd rather not acknowledge. And were he to give those other aspects full voice, his thinking, to be sound, would have to change dramatically.

The example of Hitler is so stark that it helped me to reflect on my own indifference. He caused me to wonder whether I ever use my own thought processes, presumptions, and unwillingness to understand as a way of becoming apathetic or indifferent.

This indifference toward the Jews creates the internal conditions in which Hitler can express contempt for God. For Steiner's Hitler next launches an assault on the idea of an all-seeing, invisible, omnipotent God who demands our unconditional loyalty. Hitler argues that the pagan deities are much more desirable; because humans have created them in their own image, they embody human desire. This makes the pagan gods far more humane than the God of the Jews. Hitler believes that an all-seeing, invisible, omnipotent God is the most cruel theological idea in history. The Jews have made God inaccessible to human senses. Because he is imageless, the God of the Jews cannot even be imagined. Hitler believes cruelty is compounded by the ever-present nearness of this God. And because he is all-seeing, he spies on our every motive and action. The Jewish God habitually practices blackmail. As far as Hitler is concerned, nothing could be more unfair to the human race.

Like with his first argument, Steiner's Hitler conveniently ignores certain things about God. He is indifferent to the fact that this all-seeing, omnipotent God might offer benefits to his children that far exceed the limitations or constraints to which Hitler so spitefully objects. It never occurs to Hitler that the God of the Jews, for all his awesome power, might still be accessible for human communion. He refuses to recognize that instead of receiving gifts, we might instead receive the Giver. Nor does it dawn on him that the Giver himself might enable the deepest, most profound, and most satisfying reflection. Hitler ignores the possibility that devotion to God might make us better people, exceeding all limitations. So God searches our motives. Might this not be good, in spite of its difficulties? Is it not also true that without difficulties, we will never become better people, more fulfilled and happier? Biologists have known for years that without challenges and stressors, we shrivel up. Mere comfort is good for no one. And the quest for absolute comfort is scarcely worthy of our humanity. Hitler complains that thinking about an imageless God exceeds the natural powers of the human mind. But he ignores the possibility that God's grace will more than compensate for this difficulty, lifting us above ourselves and our own limited abilities. He also ignores the possibility that our devotion to God may render us able to recognize truths that are otherwise inaccessible. Is not devotion to truth its own reward?

In Hitler's third argument he objects to the Jewish idea of self-sacrifice. His rationale? People are sick of the cry for sacrifice to truth and justice. People are weary of patience, and they want justice here and now. Moreover, the idea of the absolute creates terror in the hearts of people.

Adolf Hitler's conclusion is simple: for these reasons, he turned on the Jews. And for these reasons, he was justified in venting the Wrath of the Holocaust. Hitler even points to the Sloth of others in an effort to justify his cruelty: No one came to the rescue of the Jews. Moreover, he says, those who refused to assist the Jews were quietly thankful for Hitler's final solution — the death camps.

Notice what Steiner has accomplished. In a few short pages he has allowed us to explore Hitler's character. He has shown us Adolf Hitler taking the offensive in his own defense. He presents Hitler as entirely adversarial. And because this Hitler is so indifferent not only to the humanity of the Jews, but also to truth itself, his thought processes convey no evidence of inquiry, reflection, or seeking to understand someone else. This Hitler satisfies himself with half-truths and incomplete truths. This is *mis*representation — using *part* of the truth to stand for the *whole* truth, producing complete untruth.

George Steiner's Adolf Hitler fascinated me. In normal circumstances, we are not cruel to the degree of Nazi soldiers. But the example of Hitler is so stark that it helped me to reflect on my own indifference. He caused me to wonder whether I ever use my own thought processes, presumptions, and unwillingness to understand as a way of becoming apathetic or indifferent. Over the years I have taken great pride in rigorous analysis and thinking. I now wondered, Have I become arrogant? Have I somehow substituted logic, analysis, and rigor for thoughtful reflection? And in so doing, have I become indifferent to the tenderness and humanity of others? How do other people experience me? What impact do I make? How have I been helpful?

Steiner has shown us how perverse thinking, poisoned by Sloth, creates conditions of Sloth that make us ripe for belligerence. We can become so hostile to what we regard as distasteful that we think it our martyred right to pick and choose the (pseudo) truths to which we joylessly adhere. Do we then use half-truths and outright falsehoods to manipulate the moods and appetites of others by pandering to their indifference? Hitler did this, and he did so knowingly. He appealed to what was most base in his audience. He exploited their own propensity to Slothful pseudothinking to his own advantage. In so doing, he justified his own Wrath, all the while luring his listeners to such indifference toward our common humanity that they would entirely concede to the most diabolical apathy and carry out his cruelty.

# VIRTUAL FEELINGS

*The thoughts of their hearts are too paltry to be sinful.*
— Søren Kierkegaard, *A Kierkegaard Anthology*

I T IS SEDUCTIVE, scintillating, and addictive. And it's a virtual world. It's called The Sims. It is a video game like no other. It is not being played by children or teenagers. It is played by adults. Bob Simon, of *60 Minutes,* reported that over 60 percent of the people now playing video games are over eighteen years of age. And the average player is in his or her late twenties.

You can play The Sims using the World Wide Web. What you do is to create a virtual character that becomes you. You then use the Web to enter a virtual world, and you "interact" with other virtual characters created by other people who are also playing The Sims at their own computer terminals somewhere else in the world. This virtual world seems so real that players can easily forget that it isn't. This allows players to become immersed in a world that is completely temporary and partially real at best. And the players can do so with mutual anonymity, entirely without commitments. According to Will Wright, one of the creators of The Sims, the average player plays the game twenty hours per week. Most of the players are women.

So what are the men playing? A company on Long Island, called Acclaim Entertainment, has produced a video game called BMX XXX. The name speaks for itself. The makers of

BMX XXX have created a virtual strip club. Players of the game will see hookers and pimps. A player can even carry a hooker from one point to another in the game. It turns out that this type of video game is a part of the fastest growing segment of the market.

Why are people playing these games? Why are they becoming so addicted? And why in such high numbers? Anyone can guess and come close to the mark. Video games are a diversion. They enable people to *escape reality.* They make it possible for us to "get away from it all." People who play the games for long periods of time become mesmerized.

I'd like to focus not so much on reason or motive here, but on the *result.* But in so doing, I'd like first to offer a disclaimer. I am not suggesting that video games in particular or entertainment in general is demonic, to be avoided altogether. And I am in no way opposed to fun, games, and amusement. I do believe it to be self-evident that if entertainment is enjoyed in moderation, it enhances life. Life should be fun — some of the time. Ben Franklin's phrase "All work and no play makes Jack a dull boy" is still apt. But he, with a good many other Founders, would be less than impressed with those who want a life of all play and all escape all of the time. When a virtual world becomes our obsession, then we have a problem. I also believe that there are forms of entertainment that should be avoided altogether. Those are the kinds that — like cocaine — are inherently addictive.

What I'd like to address here is the Sloth that results from addiction to these kinds of games. *The problem is that prolonged, anonymous fantasizing leads to Sloth.* That is because we knowingly engage in pseudo-relationships, with pseudo-commitments, in complete anonymity. And much that we do in some of these virtual worlds would otherwise embarrass us were we to be found out. Prolonged disengagement compromises our humanity by diverting us from one of the most rewarding realities of human life — relationships. Relationships are one of the things in life that produce genuine joy. But to be authentic, relationships require the deep, personal commitment. Relationships are rarely easy. You have to be there to interact; you have to be fully present and accounted for. Christians have known for centuries that accountability lies near the heart of the faith. We are at our noble best when we are most accountable. Anonymity may prove invaluable when it comes to service and good works. Jesus knew what he was doing when he taught us to give alms without fanfare — without calling attention to ourselves. That is because calling attention to our good works is anything but selfless. We fail in our humanity when our sole or primary motive for giving is to gain recognition.

The problem is that prolonged, anonymous fantasizing leads to Sloth.

Accountability helps us when we are up to no good and tempted to hide our actions. We know we're up to no good when a healthy, well-developed conscience tells us so. Then, it is in our best interest to *fess up;* to give an account of who we are and what we're up to with a loving, supportive mentor who cannot be conned — a mentor who will receive us with grace while refusing to compromise in requiring *our utmost for God's highest* (to use Oswald Chambers's extraordinary phrase).

If I immerse myself in a virtual world for long periods of time, what happens to me? Do I create conditions in which Sloth can thrive? What happens when I involve myself in virtual actions that I wouldn't be caught dead doing for real? Will the line that separates reality from fantasy become so blurred that I am unable to distinguish right from wrong, and constructive from destructive?

I was talking about these computer games with two friends. One, a teenage boy, immediately responded with the story about a friend. One of the friend's favorite games is called Grand Theft Auto. Apparently, the name fits the game. All rules go out the window. In this virtual world, one practices deception and steals a car. The point of the story was that the teenager who plays this game spends well over twenty hours per week at his computer. When his computer is not working, the boy is in a state of panic. And he doesn't have much by way of social skills. His reclusiveness goes beyond what my companion considers normal. The other friend told us about a different friend of his, a man who can become so absorbed in a video game that he will play all night. Only the rising of the morning sun rouses him out of his stupor.

These two stories helped me. They raised the question, When have I crossed the line from active caring to willful indifference? And if I become indifferent, have I undermined my own ability to function and to sustain meaningful relationships? Have I somehow undermined or debilitated my own dignity and humanity? What my young friends recognized reinforced my sense of the importance of being fully awake — truly present and accounted for.

# DATE RAPE DRUG

*The line separating good and evil passes neither through states, nor between political parties either — but right through every human heart.* — Aleksandr Solzhenitsyn, *The Gulag Archipelago*

I SAT WITH A GROUP of college students. I was interested in knowing the greatest challenges they faced socially. Without hesitating, they gave me the following scenario:

First date. Beer, pizza, and a video. Because they're both away at college, they're living on a shoestring. It's just plain cheaper to pick up a pizza and a six-pack of beer and go to his dorm room than to go to a multiplex. Besides, she's been to his room before. His dorm is right next to hers.

She makes herself comfortable. He serves up the pizza and beer. What she does not realize, and what she never thought to anticipate, is that he has slipped a small white tablet into her beer. The tablet is scored on one side with the word "ROCHE," with an encircled "one" (specifying the dosage) on the other. The tablet is a drug. It's called Rohypnol. Dissolved in a drink, it is tasteless and undetectable.

What do we know about Rohypnol? It is prescribed as a sleeping pill in countries outside the United States. In the States it is illegal and must be smuggled in by mail or delivery services. In countries where it is sold legally, it is prescribed as a short-term treatment for insomnia or as a sedative hypnotic and preanesthetic. Its psychological effects are similar to Valium, but some ten times more potent. Rohypnol is a low-cost drug — approximately five dollars per tablet.

What are its effects? Rohypnol impairs judgment and motor skills. It causes disinhibition (loss of social inhibition). Its effects begin within thirty minutes, and they peak at two hours. Rohypnol incapacitates the victim's ability to resist. Taken in combination with alcohol, it affects memory and judgment. Some young women have been known to black out for a full twenty-four hours after ingestion. Other adverse effects include decreased blood pressure, drowsiness, visual disturbance, dizziness, confusion, gastrointestinal disturbances, and urinary retention.

So what is this "date" all about? It's about rape. He is completely uninterested in her. He doesn't seek to know her as a human being. He has no relationship in mind. This particular young man is interested in sex — right here, right now. What struck me about such a young man's behavior is his Sloth; his indifference and apathy are shocking. How else could he treat a young woman this way were his apathy not militant? His behavior is a charade. His refusal to embrace her dignity — her absolute preciousness as a human being — has poisoned his every motive.

I am not suggesting that the lad has no goodness whatsoever in his heart. Some of the most insightful words I have read came from Aleksandr Solzhenitsyn, describing his conversion experience. It happened when he was in a gulag in Siberia, lying on rotting straw. Solzhenitsyn had an epiphany. He was face to face with one of the fundamental truths of our humanity. Solzhenitsyn saw that the line separating good from evil runs not between countries or classes or cities or political parties, but right through the human heart. And it oscillates. He saw that even in the best of us, there remains some unpurged evil; but even in the worst of us, a small corner of goodness remains.

Our lad whose motive is rape isn't completely bad. But what goodness there is in him is poisoned with Sloth. His indifference to the young woman's sovereign personhood is diabolical. And both his personal evil and his capacity for kindness, compassion, and love are, as it were, under a spell. The result is that he isn't even willing to seduce her. Instead, motivated by his own poisoned will, he incapacitates her will, completely without her consent, for the sole purpose of assaulting her.

Solzhenitsyn saw that the line separating good from evil runs not between countries or classes or cities or political parties, but right through the human heart.

Such a young man's actions are so mindless that I began to wonder how much genuine cognizance he might have about his actions. One of the first things we notice is that his complete disregard for the woman's dignity is an assault on her spirit. At the center of her humanity is her ability to say yes or no — to give or withhold consent. He is completely indifferent to her humanity. He ignores her preciousness, which is something they have in common.

I also considered that what he does to her — anesthetizing her awareness and incapacitating her will — bears some similarity to his own Sloth. Just as he is undermining her awareness by causing her to lose consciousness, he is shutting down his own consciousness by willing himself to be indifferent.

His indifference makes it possible for him to degrade her — utterly. His malice is premeditated and calculating. He has exploited her goodness and her trust. He has assaulted her. In so doing, he has undermined any tenderness, any affection, and any intimacy that might have made human interaction between them inherently rewarding — for both of them.

Reflecting on this date rape scenario, I began to see why the monks of the early Middle Ages declared Sloth to be *deadly*. Among other things, Sloth is so sinister that it creates the character defects that make date rape possible.

However, I also recognized the very thing for which the young college students who described this scenario longed — meaningful relationships. For a relationship to be authentic, the ability to say yes or no is just the beginning. Freedom from indifference creates the possibility for us to take genuine interest in each other. When the spell of Sloth is broken, we can know each other as we truly are. Then, and only then, can we care — truly and deeply.

# X Marks the Spot

*He leads me beside still waters;*
*he restores my soul.*

— Psalm 23:2

I WAS ON RETREAT with junior and senior high youth in the San Bernardino Mountains. Our group is called the Inklings. C. S. Lewis had a group by that name. His group included J. R. R. Tolkien, and the young people in the Inklings are particularly fond of Lewis and Tolkien. We named our group in honor of these two great writers. Lewis's Inklings met for reflection, and so do we.

Because the primary purpose of the Inklings is reflection, I wanted to help the group begin to ponder just what reflection is all about. So in one of our sessions, I asked a question: "Would you rather look at your reflection in a mirror or in a pool of water outdoors in the mountains?" The group grew thoughtful. They had never been asked this question.

Finally, a girl raised her hand. "I'd prefer the pool of water."

I asked her why that was so.

She wasn't entirely sure, but she struggled to answer. "The reflection in the pool would look different. I guess it would be softer. I just think I would look better."

A deep silence entered the group. After a time I asked, "Well, what's the difference?"

Sometimes, these questions are hard to answer. But to deepen reflection and to create a climate where learning can take place, I will occasionally compose a story. Here's one I wrote for the Inklings. Among other things, it's about the subject of reflection. I entitled the story "X Marks the Spot."

*Timothy could not have described his depression, nor would he have wanted to. Medication might have helped, but he wasn't about to wait for a prescription. And he had no energy to seek help anyway — at least, not beyond what he would receive from drugs.*

*This did not discourage Lola, his youth counselor, from urging him to come to camp. "I'll kidnap you, if that's what it takes." He wasn't entirely sure that she wasn't serious. But then, he wasn't thinking clearly enough to know. But he was not easily persuaded.*

*However, they make a kind of pact.*

*"There's a treasure at this camp."*

*"Where is it?"*

*"Hidden."*

*"Hidden where?"*

*"In a field."*

*"What's it doing there?"*

*"Waiting to be discovered."*

*"Has it been discovered before?"*

*"Yes."*

*"But it's still there?"*

*"Yes."*

*"You've seen it?"*

*"I've discovered it."*

*"Why didn't you take it?"*

*"I did."*

*"But it's still there?"*

*"Most certainly."*

"You stole the treasure, but it's still there?"

"It wasn't necessary to steal it. The treasure was offered."

"What do you mean, offered?"

"You'll see."

And then, of course, he saw the trap. Were he to know anything about the treasure, he'd have to go to that camp and see for himself.

"Is it hard to find?"

"Not if you know where to look."

"Will you tell me where to look?"

"I'll give you a clue."

"How about a map?"

"My clues will be enough."

"How many clues will you give me?"

"Two."

"Can you tell me now what the clues are?"

"Will you remember them? It wouldn't hurt to write them down."

"You mean like Dr. Jones?"

"Had Dr. Jones not written down his clues, do you think Indiana would have been able to help him find the Grail?"

"I'll get a piece of paper."

"Dr. Jones didn't use a piece of paper. The clues were much too important for that. Go and buy a journal — a good one. Make it one you will be proud to keep. Your greatest treasures will go there."

"Will you give me the clues?

"Get your journal, and I'll give you the clues."

He did. So she did.

"Are you ready to write down your clues?"

"I'm all ears, journal, and pen."

"Here they are. Clue number one: There is a treasure hidden in the field. Clue number two: X marks the spot."

"Indiana Jones said that X never, ever marks the spot."

"Indiana Jones was wrong, wasn't he?"

The lad couldn't resist going to camp. As he would later admit, it was a good thing. During the first two days of camp, his search for the treasure was somewhat casual. He just sauntered around and perused the camp, hoping that the treasure would come into focus — like a three-dimensional poster. That was not to be.

It was after the second evening that his search for the treasure took on a sense of urgency that he had never known before. It wasn't that he had never felt desperate. When his brother died, he felt more desperate than he would likely feel again in his life. This was different. This was a desperation born of eager, greedy, almost panicky hope. In response, Lola thought it time to tell her story. It was the story of her moment of truth, the story of her discovering the treasure. It was the story of why this camp was incomparably important to her.

She told of losing her boyfriend. She hadn't really wished for his death. Her love for him was almost excessive. She realized in retrospect that she was too clingy because she was a little too attached.

He was taking a college class. The teacher had given the students assignments for projects. There were lots of choices. He decided to try sky diving. "It's the easiest assignment!"

"What do you mean, easiest? It'd scare me to death!"

"The whole assignment takes only three hours. You take your instruction, you go up in the plane, and you make your jump."

"He wasn't about to take No for an answer. I told him, 'I hope you kill yourself!'"

She told them, "He did. His chute wouldn't open. He couldn't get his emergency chute open in time. He fell to his death. His death was followed by the blackest depression you can imagine. I didn't want to live, but I couldn't die. I didn't have the energy to end my life.

"And then, somebody brought me to camp. It was at this camp that I found the treasure. It was hidden, here, in a field. It was in that treasure that I found the source of healing that would soothe my pain and give me new life."

That was it. He had to find the treasure now.

He couldn't sleep that night. It was too dark to look, but that didn't prevent him from trying. He sneaked out with flashlight in hand. Lola had already instructed his cabin counselor, "Let him go. He won't get into trouble. And I guarantee he won't stray from the camp."

Timothy searched into the wee hours of the morning, but without success. When he got out of his sleeping bag after just a couple of hours' sleep to resume his restless hunt, he spotted Lola, sitting on a log in the fire circle at the camp. He joined her silence. They said nothing to each other, and for the first time he knew the communion of souls. She had shared the most tender moments of the story of her own failure. He had received it with a grateful respect at the borderland of a reverence that is reserved solely for God.

It was as they walked together to the dining room that he heard the hollow thump. He noticed it as they walked. The sound under their feet was suddenly different. It's not that Timothy was listening to the sound under his feet as he walked. He simply noticed when the sound ceased to be solid. The curiosity this provoked was at first almost past the horizon of awareness. But something told him to investigate. So he kicked aside some of the dirt and found that it covered a piece of plywood. When he got the layer of dirt off the plywood, he saw the X. It was a fading black. The plywood was square; the X touched each of the four corners of the board.

"X marks the spot?"

"But X isn't the treasure. You'll have to lift the board to see what's underneath."

He almost couldn't believe that he had finally found it. Had it been completely by accident, or was she guiding him?

*Together, they lifted the plywood. When it was off, he looked downward. "It's a well." The water itself was so dark that he couldn't possibly tell how deep it was.*

*"Yes, it is."*

*"This is the treasure?"*

*"This is the treasure."*

*Timothy stared hard.*

*"It's not a 3-D picture. You don't have to look deeply, yet. Begin at the surface."*

*Timothy struggled. Nothing made sense at first. But after a few moments of tense, urgent searching, he caught it. The water was perfectly still. Looking up from it was a reflection of himself, bathed in the golden light of the rising sun. But it wasn't precisely himself. His reflection was softer, more natural. His reflection blended in, not only with the water, but with the rest of the surroundings gently depicted in the water. Not only was his reflection softer and more natural, but his pain had blended in with the world that had so kindly received him.*

AFTER I READ THE STORY to the Inklings, we spent some time pondering in silence. Our reflection began to unfold in dialogue. What was Lola doing with Timothy? She was showing him the treasure hidden in a field. He was that treasure. Lola was helping him to see himself reflected in the eyes of God. She was helping Timothy see not only who he currently was, but also a transformed image of himself in a pool of still waters. What entered his consciousness was a reflection of what he was becoming — what was seeking to emerge from the depths of his soul — right then and there. We talked about dark forces that lurked in the depths of Timothy's soul. When he isolated these forces, trying to ignore them, they posed a threat; and Timothy became dangerous to himself. But once touched by the light of God, what was beneath the surface was lovingly drawn into his consciousness as a new, transformed self.

With the Inklings, I reflected on the difference between seeing our reflections in a mirror and in a pool of water somewhere in the woods. When you see your reflection in the severe light of the bathroom, your reflection is harsh. All of you is reflected back to you at once, "warts and all." We see ourselves as we are, and we frequently don't like what we see.

But in a pool we see a reflection that is miraculously modified, or transformed, by nature. The harshness is filtered out. Our reflection is more natural. We better fit our surroundings. It's not that we blend in, in the sense that we cease to be individuals. But reflected in a pool, we belong with the pool and the trees and the rich blue sky and the soft light that is reflected in the pool. Our reflection in the pool also appears deeper than our reflection in the harsh bathroom mirror. Instead of looking at ourselves critically, as we do in the mirror, we see ourselves at home in the world.

The Inklings engage in a discipline of reflection together. By discipline, I simply mean a deliberate way of interacting with God and one another. We do spend time drawing into our awareness and dialogue things that matter. Things that matter may include a piece of great literature, a passage from the Bible, a work of art, or a situation in which we find ourselves. The situation usually involves a challenge — perhaps a conflict that needs resolution. How, then, do we reflect? We hold both our circumstances and the idea or work of art we are considering together in our consciousness. We are aware of both at once — simultaneously. As we talk, we move back and forth between emphasizing our awareness of our circumstances and the idea or image that we are considering. We look to see how each aspect is reflected in the other. We ask how each interprets the other. We imagine how each might affect and change the other. We also ponder the question, What is trying to emerge in our dialogue? How is God trying to shape us, transform us, help us grow, and make us whole? How is God making us more complete, more fully human? We listen to each other. And we listen for the Voice of the Genuine in each other and in our dialogue. We share our struggles. But as we do so, we keep a disciplined eye toward our own responsibilities in our struggles. We work at avoiding blaming others. Instead, we actively seek to forgive. We seek to learn. We reflect together on what we are supposed to do, both as a community and as individuals. We inquire as to our duties. What are we obligated to do for God? What does God require of his children? How does God call us to learn, to love, and to act? What is the Presence of God trying to think in us?

Finally, we hold each other accountable for any indifference. We work at recognizing that indifference and apathy are deadly. Sloth poisons our relationships and undermines our humanity. We try to be aware that one of the worst things that can happen to us is to become uncaring toward each other as persons and indifferent to truth. All this while trying to maintain a covenant of sustained reflection. It isn't easy. We can become pretty frustrated at times. But we have found it to be self-evident that the rewards are worth the perseverance.

# THE GREAT TEACHER

*People do not learn from experience; they learn from reflection
and interpretation.* — Louise Cowan, *Classic Texts*

E VERY ONCE IN A WHILE, I read something that rings true.
The meaning may be obvious at first reading. Or the
meaning may require a lot of thought on my part. But either
way, I know it to be something worth remembering and return-
ing to again and again. Two people whose writing has enriched
my life are Donald and Louise Cowan. Before their retirement
they were with the University of Dallas. Donald was president,
and Louise was professor of English literature. They are in large
part responsible for my falling in love with poetry as an object
of reflection.

I was sitting with a book that they had edited and for which
they had written extensively. Much of what they had written rang true for me. This included a remark about *experience*.
There is a proverb that says something to the effect that "experience is the Great Teacher." The Cowans offered a subtle, but
insightful, correction. They said, "Experience isn't the Great
Teacher. *Reflection* on experience is the Great Teacher." We
have experiences. And many of us learn nothing from the experiences that we have. That is because we don't take time,
afterward, to reflect. We learn when we reflect. We learn when
we return to our experiences, and ponder, evaluate, and seize
the opportunity to grow.

The Cowans' comments made such a strong impression on me that I became interested in reflection as a discipline. I wanted to know something about the nature of the kind of reflection that leads to learning. What is the meaning of reflection? Is the discipline of reflection worth describing? And if so, where would I begin?

What occurred to me, as I pondered the Cowans' remarks, is that if I were to understand something about reflection, I would have to begin with *consciousness*. Reflection takes place in consciousness. Consciousness is, as it were, the classroom in which reflection takes place. When we reflect, we are drawing things into our consciousness for pondering, contemplation, and reverie. That being the case, consciousness is a good place to begin the study of reflection.

Fortunately, consciousness is not difficult to describe. It is a simple phenomenon. And remarkably, consciousness is as magnificent and extraordinary as it is common.

We can understand consciousness by comparing it to the operations of our bodies. Our bodies function according to the laws of nature. If I run headfirst into a brick wall, I will hurt myself — badly. My body is subject to the same natural laws as the rest of the world. The internal structures and processes of my body are under natural law.

In addition, much of my body's operation is autonomic. My heart goes on beating, I go on breathing, and for the most part, I am completely unaware of the fact. It isn't too difficult to imagine how awful it would be if I had to remind my heart to beat, or if I constantly had to remind myself to breathe. Thank God that these autonomic processes operate according to the laws of nature and without my awareness and effort.

But there are other things that happen because of me that are neither autonomic nor strictly a part of nature. There is a *self,* an *I* that determines to a substantial degree what my body will do. *I* drive my body. *I* make decisions. *I* get up in the morning and decide what *I* will do. *I* make choices. *I* go to work. *I* take my family to dinner. *I* engage in conversation. *I* read. *I* write. *I* take our dog for a walk. And *I* reflect.

This *I* includes consciousness. Consciousness is the seat of my attention. Consciousness involves mindfulness. When I am conscious, I am awake and aware. I direct my awareness. This involves paying attention — either to the sensory world or the world of ideas, images, and intuitions. I am conscious of things when they "come to mind," and I hold them there. Consciousness is the attentive container for pondering, con-templation, and reverie. It is self-evident that it is not good to lose consciousness, for then we lose control. Consciousness is necessary for us to give and withhold consent. Making choices involves the will, which certainly seems to be related closely to consciousness. But we cannot choose wisely without being attentive, mindful, and aware.

I have an easier time understanding consciousness if I imag-ine my study at home. It is furnished with a cherrywood library table flanked by bookshelves. I also have two chairs and one of those nifty laptop "desks" and a grand piano. On the wall are some icons, a reproduction of Raphael's *The School of Athens,* and a drawing of Jiminy Cricket. My books include my Bible, my journal, Homer, Shakespeare, Wordsworth, Dante, and others. I go into my study first thing every morning. There I pray, I reach for a book, I think, and I write.

Consciousness is like my study. Just as I sit in my study and reach for a book, so do I welcome ideas, images, and circum-stances into consciousness. I cannot be mindful of everything at once. But I can be mindful of at least two or three matters at once. Reflection involves giving my attention to two or more matters and allowing an inner dialogue to take place in my consciousness. I allow these ideas, images, feelings, and desires to interact — to play off each other. I may look at them individually. I may allow them to interpret and influence each other. One idea may question or even critique another. Something new may emerge. Perhaps I will enter a quiet reverie, a kind of internal bliss. Consciousness is the place where I enjoy curiosity, wonder, and insight — that extraordinary experience of *aha!*

There is a proverb that says something to the effect that "experience is the Great Teacher." The Cowans offered a subtle, but insightful, correction. They said, "Experience isn't the Great Teacher. *Reflection* on experience is the Great Teacher."

One of my most helpful, satisfying reflections took place while I was in my study. I had been pondering a personality characteristic of mine — spontaneity. For better or for worse, God did not shortchange me when parceling out the spontaneity genes. I have them in abundance. Sometimes ideas, humor, inklings, and intuitions will come out of nowhere. They are wont to explode and gush out of me like Old Faithful.

Spontaneity can be an immeasurably good and joyous quality. It can certainly add creativity, newness, and fun to my life and the lives of others. And it also enables me to help people who are somehow stuck and can't find fresh ideas, answers, and ways of looking at things.

But spontaneity can also be my Achilles' heel. My strength can be my weakness. We spontaneous types are not naturally persistent and consistent. And this can prove difficult for others when we are in positions of leadership. Sometimes those for whom we are responsible depend on their leader's feet being planted firmly on the ground. There are occasions that call for the steady hand of methodical, reasoned judgment.

I was sitting in my study pondering my spontaneity while reading Homer's *Odyssey*. I noticed an obvious difference between Odysseus, the hero in Homer's epic, and a Cyclops, named Polyphemus, who is one of Odysseus's adversaries. The obvious difference is this: Odysseus has two eyes, and the Cyclops has one eye. Among other things, this means that Odysseus is *binocular,* and Polyphemus is *monocular.* What does it mean to be monocular? It is to be so single-minded that one suffers with what we call tunnel-vision. When I am monocular, I can see or think about one thing only. For example, if our dog, Daisey, sees me pick up her leash, she is completely overcome with excitement about going for a walk. She can't think about anything else. Going for a walk becomes her one and only obsession. And she will run in circles and bark until I put the leash on her and go out the door. That is like being monocular. The monocular see one thing, and one thing only.

But Odysseus has two eyes; he is binocular. This is one of the characteristics of Odysseus's heroics. He learns to see everything at least twice. He learns to have second thoughts. Odysseus may have a spontaneous idea. It may come out of nowhere as a seeming inspiration. But instead of acting upon it instantly, he will return to that idea. He will ponder it. He will mull it over. He will have *second thoughts.* In a word, he will *reflect.*

So there I sat, in my study, reading Homer. I was pondering the difference between the monocular tunnel vision of the one-eyed Cyclops and the binocular second thoughts of the two-eyed human. And in my own consciousness, I made a connection between what Odysseus learned about his spontaneity and how that related to my own. Odysseus's spontaneity was both a blessing and a curse. It was a curse when he acted on impulse. But it became a blessing when he learned to have second thoughts — to reflect, to think things over.

I began to reflect with Homer. I drew into consciousness my own spontaneity, with its strengths and weaknesses. I thought about circumstances where my spontaneity was helpful. More important, I thought about what I needed to learn. Odysseus provided the answer. I needed to become binocular. I needed to learn to have second thoughts. I needed to return to my spontaneous impulses and ponder them, put them to the test, and discern their helpfulness. I recognized that this would require effort at first. My having second thoughts was not first nature. It would take time for second thoughts to become second nature — that is, habitual. But in reflection, the insight came to me. I welcomed into the *room of my consciousness* a personal characteristic, circumstances, and an image and idea from great literature. And I allowed an internal dialogue to unfold between them. I called to my attention personal experiences and situations. And I saw analogies between my own experiences — including successes and failures — with those of Odysseus. In a word, I began to reflect. Moreover, I sustained reflection. I worked at hanging in there with my ponderings. And when I did so, the insight presented itself as a welcome, long-sought answer. I could begin my journey to taking a second look at my own life and circumstances — to habitual second thoughts.

By reflecting on experience, I could learn to become more fully human. What I also discovered was that when I had struggled with tunnel vision, I had become indifferent to the impact of my own spontaneity. And this was due to my own Sloth. Spontaneity had become so much a part of me that I wasn't giving sufficient attention to its consequences. What I needed was not so much to have my spontaneity exorcised as to make spontaneity my friend. A good friend doesn't possess us. A good friend doesn't absorb our attention so much that we become indifferent and apathetic to the impact we make on others. A good friend will share strengths, but with gracious limits. A good friend, like a great teacher, will even become a partner in reflection.

# Music and Beauty

*Praise him with trumpet sound;*
*praise him with lute and harp!*
*Praise him with tambourine and dance;*
*praise him with strings and pipe!*
— Psalm 150:3–4, NRSV

My wife, Nancy, and I were driving with our friend Shirley to Cedar Breaks, a National Monument in Utah, forty-five minutes from Cedar City, Utah. We were attending the annual Shakespearean Festival, and we wanted also to enjoy the beautiful mountains and trees. As we approached the Monument, we noticed that nearly a third of the trees were dead. I asked the park ranger the cause of their death. She said that there were two causes, which taken together were lethal. One was a drought. The trees were just plain thirsty, starved for nourishment. The other was the spruce bark beetle. The beetles had infested the Older Engelmann spruce trees. When the beetles were in smaller numbers, the spruce could resist them. But what with an infestation *and* a lack of water, many of the trees had no immunity. Some had died. Others were struggling.

I reflected on the similarity between humans and the Older Engelmann spruce. The spruce requires a certain level of nourishment not only to thrive, but to survive. What kinds of nourishment do we need? Just as the tree emerges and unfolds from a seed, taking firm root and ever reaching for the light of the sun, what is required for us? What is the *water* that human consciousness drinks in and reflects upon? Are there certain things that we are to avoid? Or better, are there matters that the mind can handle, but only within limits and moderation? Are there stimuli that can infest and kill the human spirit?

I remembered another gift of beauty that came to me from Utah. A friend named Paul, an organist, teacher, and lover of music, had introduced me to the work of Michael Ballam, an opera singer and professor of music in Utah. One of the gifts that Ballam has given the world is both a genuine love of music and an understanding of how music and the mind fit, how they belong together. Ballam has reflected carefully about the impact of beauty on the human mind.

Ballam loves to tell stories of laboratory research involving music. As I listen to him and read his reports, I see that these are not the sterile, boring reports of tedious, mundane lab work. Ballam senses the unfolding of mystery, which emerges right there in the lab. He senses that what happens in the laboratory opens a window to a larger mystery. Three of the researchers whose story he likes to tell are C. A. Hardy, B. Stein, and H. L. Totten, of the University of North Texas. The year was 1982. Hardy, Stein, and Totten tried an experiment. They began by gathering a group of PhDs in a university classroom where they taught the academics vocabulary words. One researcher would write a word on the board and define it. After all the words had been listed and defined, the researchers administered an examination, testing the recall of the group that had learned the words. The researchers then taught the same words to a second group of PhDs. The instruction was identical to that employed with the first group. The number of PhDs learning the words was the same for both groups. However, one variable in the teaching process changed for the second group. The first group listened to the definitions of the words to a background of silence. The second group, on the other hand, was taught to the background of G. F. Handel's *Water Music*.

Like the first group, the second was examined immediately following the instruction. But their results were dramatically different. Those who learned with *Water Music* filling their consciousness retained far more than those who learned in silence. This result so startled the researchers that they regathered all the participants two weeks later and retested both groups. They discovered that the disparity between levels of retention was even greater. The group that learned to Handel's music remembered a great deal more than the group that learned in silence.

In 1988, other researchers, Gervasia M. Schreckenberg (a neurobiologist at Georgian Court College) and Harvey H. Bird (a physicist at Fairleigh Dickinson University) conducted a similar experiment. But instead of using PhDs, they used mice! The researchers first recorded the amount of time it took a group of mice to learn their way through a maze in silence. They then recorded the amount of time the mice required to learn, not to the sound of Handel's *Water Music*, but to Strauss's waltzes. The second group of mice learned far more rapidly than the first. But the researchers didn't stop there. A third group of mice learned the maze to the sound of heavy metal rock music. The results were dramatic; this group took the longest to learn the maze, seeming to the researchers to become increasingly disoriented and confused. At the conclusion of the experiment, the researchers performed autopsies on the mice's brains. They discovered that the mice that were exposed to a continuous barrage of rock music had developed abnormal neurons in the hippocampus, the part of the brain associated with alertness, learning, and memory. They did not, however, find the growth of abnormal neurons in the mice that were exposed either to silence or Strauss's music. The researchers also discovered that the mice learning to the sound of heavy metal music suffered disruptions in the normal amounts of messenger RNA, a chemical that facilitates the storage of memories. Schreckenberg and Bird believe that the mice were trying to compensate for the constant bombardment of disharmonic noise that made a toxic neurological impact on their nervous systems.

If we are to thrive, we can't get stuck in Sloth. We will need to overcome our indifference. For this to happen, we need sufficient beauty. Beauty provides essential nourishment to our consciousness. It gives us resources for reflection. This is because beauty is an expression of the order of life.

Ballam reports other experiments for which he does not provide dates. A high school student from Suffolk, Virginia, conducted a similar experiment for his science fair project. This student allowed his mice to run a maze for ten minutes. He then divided the mice into two groups. The first group listened to classical music for ten hours a day, the second to heavy metal music. In three weeks' time, the mice exposed to classical music made it through the maze in one and a half minutes. The mice exposed to rock music took thirty minutes. The experiment came to an end when all of the hard rock mice killed each other.

Another scenario features neither mice nor people, but plants. A Dr. Singh, from India, conducted an experiment whereby he observed and measured the growth of plants. In addition to plants that grew in silence were plants that Dr. Singh exposed to lute music. Those that grew to the lute music grew 20 percent faster and produced 72 percent more leaves. Michael Ballam also reports that a plant experiment was conducted at the University of Colorado. A group of plants was exposed to hard rock music. These plants grew abnormally tall and then died in two weeks. Other plants that were exposed to baroque and classical music leaned toward the speakers. Moreover, plants exposed to music by Bach leaned sixty degrees toward the speakers, and those plants that were close enough to do so wrapped themselves around the speakers.

What was the music doing to the participants? Ballam's suggestion is insightful: classical and baroque music express a certain *order*. This order is similar to both the order of the human mind in particular and the order of the universe in general. This is why humans, animals, and plants *resonate* with baroque and classical music. People, plants, and animals drink this orderliness from the music. And when they do so, they function better, and they learn.

My sense is that Ballam is on to something — that the order in classical and baroque music fits the order of the human mind. Perhaps the order is identical; music and the mind may go hand in hand. Or perhaps it is reciprocal; it may be that they fit hand in glove. Perhaps the order in the music is even like a sock — one size fits all. In other words, perhaps the order in the music is sufficiently elastic and malleable that it stretches, or fits, but without losing its form, function, or character.

I once told a group of young people about Michael Ballam's work. As we reflected together, one of the girls asked, "Does this mean I should never listen to hard rock?" I asked in response, "Can you enjoy hard rock in moderation? Can you set limits? And are you willing to give some care to filling your mind with music, art, and literature that will enable you to respond to beauty, to think, to listen to yourself and God, to reflect, and to learn?" The young people thought this worth pondering. Another way to put it is this: What can emerge in my reflections when I am bathed in hard rock, classical music, or sheer silence?

When I think about music and human consciousness, I reflect back on those Older Engelmann spruce trees. They need a sufficiently healthy immunity to beetles. They also need plenty of nourishment to grow. Michael Ballam found this to be true of human consciousness as well. If we are to thrive, we can't get stuck in Sloth. We will need to overcome our indifference. For this to happen, we need sufficient beauty. Beauty provides essential nourishment to our consciousness. It gives us resources for reflection. This is because beauty is an expression of the order of life. So are goodness and truth. They are expressions of life's nobility. Goodness, beauty, and truth nourish the human spirit just as protein, fruits, vegetables, and carbohydrates nourish our bodies. When I eat more or less properly, my body functions better, especially when I get plenty of exercise and sleep. Similarly, when I take sufficient beauty into my consciousness, I function better — mentally and spiritually. I am able to think more clearly.

This is far different from "chilling out," so that my emotions are "mellow," and I can better "cope." Taking beauty, goodness, and truth into my consciousness helps me to organize my imagination so I can reflect on the circumstances that I face, along with their conflicts, challenges, and opportunities to grow.

I HAVE A FRIEND named Jim. He is a successful plaintiff's lawyer. He is quite familiar with the pressures associated with his law firm and the challenge of serving his clients and securing justice. How does he find the balance that he knows he needs? Jim has a healthy appetite for reflection through dialogue. He recognizes this as a legitimate spiritual need. And how does he go about meeting that need? One way is by developing small discussion groups. Jim and I recently put together a group of half a dozen people in our congregation. We meet regularly for lunch downtown, near people's offices. Prior to each lunch, we will have read something that merits thoughtful reflection. Over lunch, we dialogue.

With his wife, Gale, Jim has put together a small group of young people from our youth group. Our youth are spread out all over Greater San Diego, but several live in Jim and Gale's neck of the woods. They draw the youth to meet regularly. Then they will do something fun together. But the fun is always followed by a dialogue. Jim often invites me to come and lead their dialogue. Invariably, the young people not only open up but they also teach me as much as I teach them.

Jim and I also have a friend named Steve. His life is filled with as much pressure as ours are. Like clockwork, when a holiday approaches, Jim and Gale invite Steve and his wife, Anne, and their family, along with the Blackwells, to their home for a barbecue. Jim knows not to overplan. The gathering consists of eating together and reflecting. The most enjoyable part is the quiet conversation.

Not too long ago, our three families gathered at Jim and Gale's. Each of our families had been dealing with pressure aplenty. And the meal, with its reflections, was just what the doctor ordered; it *restored our souls*. The best part was the time following the meal. Steve and Anne requested that Jim and I play the piano. Now, Jim and I are anything but accomplished musicians. But we love music, and I certainly love his Steinway. And Jim has a collection of classical music that includes piano duets. So the climax of our evening consisted of Jim and John's jammin' at the Steinway. For me, it was a gift from heaven. Because our friends are so accepting and loving, Jim and I were able to cast self-consciousness to the wind. We laughed when we made mistakes — which means that we were laughing practically the whole time! And we took sheer pleasure in the serendipity of actually playing the right notes — together, no less — from time to time. But most important for both of us, our three families enjoyed the knitting together of our souls, which tended to unravel as life pulled us in multiple, sometimes conflicted directions. The music, the meal, and our reflections were all in harmony.

# A Song's Mystery

*He was wounded for our transgressions,*
*crushed for our iniquities;*
*upon him was the punishment*
*that made us whole,*
*and by his bruises we are healed.*

— Isaiah 53:5, NRSV

I T WAS THE FIRST TIME that I studied the song in earnest.
I had been curious about it for years. It was one of those
passages in the Bible that I sensed held some great mystery. I
had made a mental note to explore it more deeply.

I spent considerable time trying to understand the song from
several angles. Suddenly (it seemed miraculous to me at the
time), I saw the answer to another puzzle that had haunted
me for years. The puzzle was inherent in a story. I was college-
aged when I first read it. I found the story in a book by Leslie
Weatherhead, a twentieth-century English Methodist preacher.
I had found Weatherhead to be a mesmerizing preacher and
writer. He opened my eyes to the study of theology. He gave
me a great hunger for learning. Leslie Weatherhead was the
kind of Christian who studied the Bible, the human sciences,
and poetry all at once. I found his insights to be stimulating
and even breathtaking.

The story he told features a young boy whose parents had
great difficulty raising the lad. They had tried everything they

knew, but it was to no avail. It seemed then, and it seems now, that their discipline was too harsh. Dr. Weatherhead reports nothing by way of what I usually think of as love. Everything the boy's parents did to him seemed to involve punishment. They took away the boy's allowance. They denied him the desserts he loved. They restricted his activities. And they beat him. But the boy's heart simply grew more and more hard. His teachers tried to improve his behavior by keeping him after school, but this didn't work either.

Something then happened between the boy and his dog. It was summer. The boy and his puppy were in the backyard, and the boy was trying to teach the dog to sit up and shake a paw. But the puppy wasn't doing very well. He wasn't learning the trick. It was hot and sticky, and the boy grew impatient. In his frustration, he kicked his puppy in the teeth. The puppy reeled over backward and hit its head on the ground. The boy then saw his puppy struggle to its feet. He looked, and he saw that the puppy was trying so hard to understand. It wanted so badly to do the trick successfully — to please its master. But its shoulder was hurt, and it couldn't lift its paw. And the boy noticed that blood was trickling from the puppy's mouth and its lip was swollen. The puppy then came to the boy and licked his hand, trying, somehow, to love the lad. And when the boy saw this, he burst into tears and ran into the house, calling to his mother, "I've done an awful thing! I've done an awful thing!"

This was the beginning of a change in the boy. The puppy's suffering melted his heart. The pain, which he alone had caused the puppy and which the puppy had suffered willingly, remaining faithful in his love for the boy, initiated a transformation. It became the beginning of the boy's healing.

That story stunned me. It seemed to contain a mystery. Dr. Weatherhead gave no clinical diagnosis. And it would be years before I was able to recognize seeds of Sloth taking root in the boy's spirit: his young heart was hardening. He wasn't becoming merely angry. His anger was somehow poisoned by apathy and indifference. But I didn't see this at first. Yet, I was deeply intrigued by the way the dog's suffering affected the boy. And I wanted to understand this impact. Finally, decades later, I *began* to understand. Having said that, I am not sure this is the sort of thing one ever understands completely.

What helped me the most was Isaiah's Song of the Suffering Servant. This was the song I was reading again in earnest. As I did so, it occurred to me that the Song, among other things, was a kind of remedy, or solution, to the problem of Sloth. I now recognized, in this song, a healing balm that melts a hard heart. Why is that? *It is because Sloth has to do with stubborn indifference and apathy, whereas the Servant Song involves thoughtful reflection.* And the reflection that the Song of the Suffering Servant describes leads to deep and lasting transformation.

It begins in Isaiah 52:13 and it ends at 53:12. The occasion of the Song involves the ending of Israel's captivity. Israel has been in exile for forty-seven years. The prophets of Israel understood that it was the fault of the people that they were in exile. Israel had worshiped everything and everyone except God. And God had warned Israel, time and again, to return to him. But it was all to no avail. Israel had become *indifferent* toward God. Finally, in the years 587 and 586 B.C., God had called Nebuchadnezzar of Babylon to destroy the temple in Jerusalem and to take the priests and the aristocracy into exile.

It was in the year 539 B.C. that Isaiah announced the end of the Babylonian exile. As he did so, he put forth a song that I find to be one of the most remarkable songs imaginable — the Song of the Suffering Servant.

The first thing that I noticed about the Song is that it unfolds in three parts. The first part is set in heaven. God is the Speaker, and the Speaker is talking about his servant who is in exile. *God is observing this servant.* The servant is marred and disfigured. His appearance is "beyond human semblance." And yet, says God, this servant shall be exalted and lifted up. He shall be held most high. Isaiah does not disclose the Servant's identity. He doesn't tell us whether the servant is one individual in exile, or the entire people of Israel. Why doesn't Isaiah tell us this? Is it because he (or God) doesn't want us to know? Is it because he (or God) wants us to wonder? Is Isaiah drawing us in — provoking our curiosity?

Isaiah makes us witnesses to God's conclusions: His righteous servant shall bear the iniquities of others. He shall do so *in their contemplation and reflections.*

Isaiah shows us God in the act of observing the reactions of the kings of the gentiles to the servant. The kings are reacting to the servant, and God is observing their reactions; the kings are baffled, stunned, astonished, and astounded. They can hardly believe what their eyes are seeing. They are completely mesmerized, totally captivated. And God observes their captivity; the kings are contemplating the suffering servant's plight, condition, behavior, and response.

In particular, God is observing the *reflections* of the gentile kings. This is what happens in the second section of the

Song. Here, with God, we readers observe the reflections of the kings as they *contemplate* the servant. They are utterly astonished. The servant's appearance is like a root sticking above the ground in a vast, parched desert — single, alone, and withered. To put it in our terms, *this servant isn't much to look at.* Nothing about him is in any way desirable. He is despised and rejected — a man of suffering whose life is riddled with grief. He is the kind of person from whom others hide their faces. They hold him in contempt; they want nothing to do with him.

As the kings reflect on this, *they notice something, and it startles them:* They are being changed. Their own reflections on the suffering servant are affecting them deeply and dramatically. This servant's willingness to suffer is penetrating the very soul of their imaginations. He is provoking them to ponder. And when they do, they discover that the servant is somehow bearing — taking in and carrying — their own sickness and sin *as they thoughtfully contemplate the servant's plight.* They reflect on how they had presumed that God had struck down the servant, only to discover that they were wrong. Their thinking was in error. They admit this freely. They recognize instead that the servant was wounded for their own transgressions. They discover that *as they reflect on this servant's suffering,* they are being made whole. The servant's bruises are somehow healing them.

The kings are so astounded that their reflection deepens. They turn inward. They discover that they themselves have gone astray, like sheep. They have turned to their own ways, their own motives, and their own forms of manipulation. This leads them to recognize that the servant was taken away by a perversion of justice. There was no deceit in him. But he was oppressed. He was afflicted with pain. Yet he made no objection, no protest. He bore the pain willingly. His suffering was an act of sovereign consent. The kings recognize that the servant was stricken for the transgressions of the kings and their subjects. And they are completely astounded. This is unlike anything they would expect.

Perhaps most astonishing, the kings entertain and reflect on the idea that it is God who is crushing his servant with pain. For what they see reflected in the suffering servant's plight is an offering for sin — their very own. In their contemplation, they discover that they are being changed and transformed, and they are prospering. Looking inward, they witness the transformation of the foundation of their own sovereign humanity.

This leads them to recognize that the suffering servant shall see light out of his anguish. He shall find satisfaction through his knowledge. And what is the suffering servant's knowledge? It is the awareness that his sovereign consent to suffering — for the benefit of others without counting cost to self — carries the capacity to transform the consciousness of those willing to take in and contemplate his suffering. *Thoughtful people will be changed to the extent that they receive, contemplate, and reflect the life of the suffering servant willingly.*

Finally, the scene in the Song shifts back to heaven. This is the third and final movement. We return to God who is still observing the reflections of the gentile kings. God now observes that the kings first thought the servant a transgressor, only to discover that the servant was interceding *for* transgressors and doing so voluntarily. And so God declares that he will allot his servant a portion with the great.

Isaiah makes us witnesses to God's conclusions: His righteous servant shall bear the iniquities of others. He shall do so *in their contemplation and reflections.* Insofar as they will embrace and ponder the suffering of this servant, the servant will transform their consciousness and make them righteous. *God has joined the servant in his suffering for the benefit of others. And God joins others in their contemplation of the suffering servant.* Consequently, they are changed; their consciousness is transformed. They are made whole — more fully human.


IT WAS IN READING the Song of the Suffering Servant that I suddenly saw the key that unlocked the mystery that had haunted me for years: The boy who kicked his puppy had been held captive under a Spell of Sloth. He was somehow indifferent, apathetic, and uncaring. The suffering of his puppy broke through that apathy and indifference. In his puppy, for the first time he saw the suffering he had caused. He saw his own brutality, lovingly reflected back to him in his own puppy, who suffered willingly — because of him and for him. His puppy's suffering penetrated the barrier of his own Sloth. And for the first time, he spontaneously cared.

What was happening here? Without realizing it, the boy was reflecting. His reflections went to the heart of his sovereign humanity. A transformation ignited in his heart as he reflected on the suffering he was causing. As he reflected, he enjoyed the spontaneous eruption of wholeness in the center of his being. The puppy's suffering disturbed him, identified him, and penetrated him. It compelled the boy to recognize himself, his puppy, and the suffering he had caused. He recognized them at once, simultaneously, as one: "I've done an awful thing!"

The Song of the Suffering Servant is our invitation to reflect on our participation in hostilities. It invites us to look at our own circumstances, including animosity we have suffered and antagonism we have caused, or perhaps are causing. Thankfully, it is rare that the conflicts we suffer approach the magnitude of those that Jesus suffered. It is also exceedingly difficult to maintain our composure when we are in the heat of hostilities.

In light of these difficulties, I noticed that what Isaiah has given us is a song. Songs, by nature, involve reflection. Music invites us to ponder. When we are reading, singing, or hearing the Song of the Suffering Servant, we do not experience the intensity of real-life interaction, with its inevitable conflicts. Yet the Song evokes feeling aplenty. It affords us the opportunity to remain sufficiently calm so as to ponder hostilities suffered *and* hostilities caused. It grants us the grace to inquire as to the kinds of people we *have been,* and the inspiration to begin to imagine what God is calling us *to be.* And with the grace *to be,* also comes the grace *to ask for forgiveness, forgive others, and begin again.*

# THE BIGGEST RISK

*This is my blood of the new covenant, which is poured out for many.* —Jesus, in Mark 14:24, NRSV

I T WAS THE EARLY 1980S. I was beginning to study the story of Jesus' crucifixion in earnest. This was the first time that I gave this story sustained reflection.

I understood little, if anything, about it. I can still remember the first flicker of insight — a mere inkling, at best. I first noticed what Jesus did in the Garden of Gethsemane, how he *responded* to his captors. The crowd came to the garden, with swords and clubs, to arrest Jesus. And at the moment when they took him, Jesus didn't resist or retaliate. He didn't respond to violence with additional violence. Jesus didn't, as we sometimes say in our culture, "stand up and fight like a man!"

But neither did Jesus run. He didn't attempt to escape, to flee the scene. Jesus didn't hide from the mob. He didn't try to protect himself.

Another way to state this would be to say that *fight* or *flight* weren't Jesus' only options.

What, then, did Jesus do? He met his captors. He *presented* himself to them. When I noticed this for the first time, I wondered, is there a kind of transformation going on here? Is Jesus somehow *transforming his own being taken captive into a giving of himself?* And in so doing, is he somehow transforming their act of taking — with malice aforethought — into an act of receiving? And if he is, what is it that they are receiving?

The second thing I noticed was that what Jesus actually *did* in response to his being taken bore remarkable similarity to what he did with the bread at his Supper. Jesus took the bread, blessed it, broke it, *gave* it to his disciples, and said, "Take, this is my body, which is given for you." I noticed that one episode reflected the other.

What happened in my reflections was this: a question began to emerge. *Did Jesus have a vocation to suffer? Was suffering — which began with transforming his own being taken captive into a giving of himself — at the heart of his calling as Son of God?* What kinds of things did Jesus ponder? There was conflict aplenty between Israel and the Romans. The Romans occupied Jerusalem. The atmosphere was always tense. Violence was a serious threat. And the Romans far outnumbered the Jews in general and Jesus' small group of followers in particular. How do people typically respond to violence? Jesus certainly would have known that some people get as far away from trouble as possible. These will just plain run. But this raises an important question: Do those who flee do anything to *resolve* the conflict? Others want to retaliate, to fight. This was true of the zealots who followed Jesus. Does this brand of zeal solve any of the problems in a lasting way?

How, THEN, might he have come to understand suffering as a *calling?* I wondered whether he wouldn't have studied the Song of the Suffering Servant in Isaiah 52–53. I reflected that Mark, in his Gospel, saw the Lord's Supper as reflecting Jesus' transformation in the Garden of Gethsemane. Might the Song of the Suffering Servant and the Crucifixion also reflect one another? Would Jesus' reflections not have included the Song?

Isaiah presents a vision of a servant suffering willingly, for the benefit of others, without counting the cost to self. What would reflecting on the Song have meant to Jesus? What would Jesus have seen? Reading the Song, Jesus would have seen the kings of the earth pondering the suffering servant in sheer astonishment. He would have seen their imaginations captivated and mesmerized. And he would have been confronted with their being changed — transformed through their reflections. Jesus would have read of people's reporting that the suffering servant's wounds were making them whole.

As I reflected on the Song and on Jesus, I realized that the Song doesn't say much about how the shedding of blood affects the consciousness of the one for whom blood is shed. I knew that the bread in the Lord's Supper reflected the way Jesus responded to his captors. But what about Jesus' blood? Can we understand something of the mystery of his words, "This is my blood of the new covenant, which is poured out for many"? How would I answer this question?

I began to reflect on what it would do to a person to receive someone's blood as a gift that bears the power to transform one's consciousness. With no disrespect to those who interpret the shedding of blood as the payment of a debt demanded by God, I did not find that explanation either satisfying or convincing. In search of some basic insight, a place to begin, I composed a story. I wanted both to learn something of the importance of Jesus' shedding of blood and to be able to convey it to others. Here is the story I composed:

*In the late 1960s a family of Vietnam refugees made their way to Camp Pendleton in California, and subsequently to Los Angeles. The family name was Nguyen. This family had a fourteen-year-old boy named Chi Nigh, who ended up attending a junior high school* in the area. Someone thoughtfully recommended that he go by the name Tony. She wanted to see him accepted by his peers, and she knew that Chi Nigh would never work in this junior high school.

Tony could not begin to express the gratitude he felt for the privilege of living in a country where he no longer needed to be afraid. It was some time before the planes landing at LAX no longer sent his heart rate skyrocketing. But in time, he learned that he need not be afraid.

The challenge for Tony was how to express his gratitude. Junior high boys just weren't in the habit of thanking each other for the joy of safety back in the late 1960s. Nor did junior high boys think it cool to hang out with Vietnamese refugees.

But there was one junior high boy who felt for Tony. His name was Tommy. And Tommy wanted, without losing face, to take Tony under his wing. This involved a wee bit of improvisation on Tommy's part. The junior high student's manual had no section on "How to Welcome a Refugee." So what Tommy did was to initially offer Tony warm greetings. He'd simply say, "Hi, Tony." And Tony would practically explode in a fit of joy and exclaim, "Hey, Tom! How do you do?" And Tommy would chuckle and reply, "Fine, Tony, how do you do?" And Tony, grinning from ear to ear, would call back, "Fine, Tom!"

That pretty much sums up the contents of their interaction. But these were junior high boys, and they were giving it their level best.

Till one day, when Tommy arrived home from school to discover that his father was already there. "Dad, how come you're home so early?"

"I got laid off."

"You mean you lost your job?"

Tommy's father was not thinking very rationally at this point. "The problem is all those damn Vietnamese. They've come into our country, and they're taking all the jobs."

Tommy was devastated.

The next day at school, Tony greeted Tommy as always: "Hey, Tom! How do you do?" But this time, Tommy practically spat, "Shut up, Nip!"

Tony was stunned and completely bewildered. He couldn't imagine what had gone wrong.

It was after school that things came to a head. Tony's path home took him across the field, past the handball courts, and into the parking lot. There, Tommy was waiting for him. This time, Tony spoke much more tentatively. "Tom, how do. . . . " He was never able to finish. The next thing he knew, Tommy had grabbed his shoulders and in a flash pulled Tony's face and shoulders sharply downward as Tommy also raised his knee, which he drove with a thud into Tony's face. Tony let out a low moan and slumped to the asphalt.

Looking down at Tony, Tommy took in three things at a glance. The first was that a small pool of blood was gathering under Tony's face. The second was that Tony raised his head to look at Tommy with swollen, pleading, tear-filled eyes. And the third was that Tony's lower lip was split, and it was from it that the blood trickled.

Softly, Tony queried his beloved assailant: "Tommy, how do you do to me? And why?"

Tommy's heart sank. He fell to his knees next to his friend, put his arms around him, and said, "Tony, Tommy is sorry. Tommy is so sorry. Tommy was bad. Tommy shouldn't have hurt you. Tommy is so wrong. I'm wrong. Please forgive me. Tommy wants to be your friend."

Gently, he lifted his friend to his feet. Tommy lived just two blocks away. He kept his arm around Tony as he led him to his house. And when they entered the kitchen, where Tommy's grieving father was sitting, Tommy said, "Dad, we've made an awful mistake."

Tommy and his father didn't realize it, but they had been headed into the abyss of Sloth. In their own pain, they were tempted to close *their eyes to what Tony and his family were also suffering. This made it possible for them to want to punish Tony and his family in an effort somehow to relieve their own pain, sadness, and misery.*

*But what they allowed themselves to see was Tony's own willingness to suffer — because of them and for them. And because Tommy was willing to see, because he was willing to reflect, he began to change — right then and there. He probably could not have explained it. But I am not sure that explanation was necessary. Tommy nevertheless knew something at the core of his own sovereignty. In Tony's suffering, he somehow bore the mystery.*

My GOAL IN COMPOSING THIS STORY was to reflect on the capacity of the willing shedding of blood to transform the consciousness of the one for whom blood is shed. Among other things, Tony somehow made his blood a direct, gracious offering to Tommy. And he did so with utter kindness. Tony was completely compassionate.

Among other things, to love means to be fully present. It may not always mean to bleed for others literally. But it does mean somehow to live our lives *for* others. Jesus understood that one's blood is one's life.

Similarly, Tommy was not indifferent to Tony, in spite of the loyalty he had for his father and the pain he was suffering with him. But in Tony's blood, which Tommy had shed, Tommy saw all the pain, injustice, misunderstanding, cruelty, and pathos in which all of them were involved together. He saw his own life, and the lives of his father, Tony, and other refugees expressly reflected in Tony's blood. As Tony's blood trickled onto the parking lot pavement, so did it flow into and occupy Tommy's consciousness. Somehow, he was changed. His eyes were opened. He saw things more completely, and he responded with love.

THERE WAS MUCH that Jesus *taught*. He told stories. And he sometimes gave directions on how to live one's life and how to follow him. But there were other times when he simply *responded* to people, not in words, but in his demeanor, behavior, and treatment of others. I don't think it is true to say that Jesus ever fled. He did withdraw from time to time. He seems to have recognized the importance of retreating for the purpose of renewing body and spirit. There were also times when he sharply criticized, and even cursed, the attitudes, teachings, and behavior of others. Jesus was no wimp. He could be tough, and sometimes he was. At one point, in the temple, he overturned tables and expelled the merchants. But it would not be correct to say that Jesus was ever violent. Jesus neither fled nor fought as a matter of design or habit.

What is clear is that Jesus *received* people. He bore them. By design and habit, he was hospitable. He welcomed people. He made room for them. This included his enemy.

To describe Jesus, we use the word "love," and well we should. This wonderful word, however, is so common that sometimes we can be a bit indifferent to its depth. One of the things it meant to Jesus was to bear people and circumstances. Among other things, to love means to be fully present. It may not always mean to bleed for others literally. But it does mean somehow to live our lives *for* others. Jesus understood that one's blood is one's life.

Jesus took a big risk. He trusted that his habitual, selfless hospitality would reflect and express God's love. He risked that offering his own life to others — directly, for their benefit, and without counting the cost to himself — would somehow transform them.

His shedding of blood for the benefit of others also comes to us as a kind of a calling. This calling has something to do with actively reflecting on how we can bear with others, in the hope that our expressions of love somehow offer the possibility of transformation. It is worth pondering how, instead of either fleeing or fighting, we might be *with* people, even in situations of conflict.

# Rabbi of Reflection

*In my own experience, I first became aware that it was God's word that was coming to me by the effects it had on myself and others around me.* — Dallas Willard, *Hearing God*

HOW DO I RECOGNIZE the Voice of God? This was the question I had begun to ponder in earnest. It not only seemed to me that nothing was *more* important, I wondered whether there was anything *as* important.

I cannot remember how I first learned about Dallas Willard's book *Hearing God*. But I do remember that I couldn't wait to get my hands on it. I poured over the pages. The purpose of the book is to help us to develop a relationship with God that is *conversational*. This means learning to *recognize God's Voice*.

Dallas Willard's words struck me for their clarity and directness. He offered three criteria — he calls them *lights* — by which we can identify the Voice of God. The first is a certain *quality*. The Voice of God will be *self-authenticating*: it will have the weight of compelling authority. The Voice of God will, as we say, *ring true*. That is because the Voice of God is the Voice of the Genuine.

The second light involves a certain *spirit*. The spirit of the Voice of God will include peace, exalted joy, deep love, and remarkable self-control. The Voice of God doesn't dazzle or overwhelm us. God doesn't express his words in the same spirit as, say, the lights and advertising on the Las Vegas Strip. The Voice of God is gentle and kind, as well as confident and firm.

Third, the Voice of God will have certain *contents*. Those contents will be in keeping with passages from Scripture such as the Ten Commandments, the Sermon on the Mount, Romans 3–8, and Philippians 2.

What I love about Dallas Willard's insights is that he teaches us that we can learn to recognize the Voice of God in our reflections. We can ponder the quality, spirit, and contents of the voices that emerge in our imaginations. We can learn to identify The Genuine.

To do this, of course, means that we have to be awake and paying attention. We cannot be Slothful. The indifferent and apathetic will not recognize the Voice of God because they won't care enough to do so.

Willard's insights helped me to organize my reflections on the voices I heard in imagination. I also found that his clear, direct teaching complemented a story I heard from my friend Paula. I treasure this story for many reasons, not the least of which is that it is about a man who heard and recognized the Voice of God when he least expected to. But the man recognized the Voice because he was willing to set aside so much of what he had carefully clung to — his own presuppositions. He was willing to recognize the Voice of the Genuine at that precise moment when the Voice spoke. Moreover, many of the things the man in the story said to Paula spoke directly of his own reflections.

It was in August 1975 that Paula lost her husband, Roy, and their daughter, Sarah, in a head-on collision that she alone survived. Paula was pregnant with their second child at the time. Because of the loss Paula has suffered in life, and the sustained reflection she has done subsequent to her loss, Paula is frequently asked to give lectures on the subject of recovery from grief. In addition she is a trained psychotherapist, and so she was asked to give an evening lecture in a government building to a completely secular gathering of therapists.

Prior to the talk, the group's leader reminded Paula that what with the separation of church and state, this was to be a completely secular enterprise. The person instructed Paula not to include any religious content in her lecture: "Please keep it clinical." Paula agreed.

She gave her lecture to the gathered participants. As instructed, Paula kept her remarks *clinical*. The talk was followed by the traditional question-and-answer session. Paula fielded several questions. A woman raised her hand and asked Paula to say something about the role of *forgiveness* in the healing enterprise. Giving her answer, Paula chose her words carefully. She said, "The role of forgiveness is pivotal." That answer was clinical.

The questioner persisted. "You have been so open with us. Would you please share with us *your story* of the role of forgiveness in your own healing and recovery from grief?"

Wanting still to obey her marching orders, Paula made a few more foggy remarks. But her questioner wouldn't back down. "I don't understand this. You have been so open with us. Please. Would you please share with us your story?"

Paula thought, "Okay, the audience has asked. I did not seek the opportunity to share my story." And Paula proceeded to share her story of loss and how it was that Christ brought her to the place where she could forgive the man who killed her husband and daughter, and how Christ had healed her. When she tells her story, it is profound because there was a time when Paula actually came face to face with the man who was responsible for the death of her husband and daughter, and she reports that between them there was only the love of God.

Sitting toward the back of the room where Paula was speaking was an older gentleman dressed in a three-piece pinstripe suit. He raised his hand and asked Paula, "This happened to you? What you just reported is true? You were not making any of it up?"

Paula replied, "That's right, sir. The story is entirely true. I didn't make it up."

Others asked questions. Then the man in the back raised his hand again and said, "Forgive me, but I just want to make sure. Everything you said is true? It was Christ who enabled you to forgive the man?"

With utter respect, Paula said, "Yes, sir. Everything that I said is true."

More questions from others followed. Finally, this same man raised his hand yet a third time. "I am sorry, but I need to make sure. You are sure that all of your story is true? The one who healed you is Christ?"

"Yes, sir. It was Christ who healed me."

At the conclusion of the question-and-answer session, people came forward to shake Paula's hand and to thank her. And the very last person in line was this man. When he approached Paula, holding out both of his hands, he took both of hers and said, "Young woman, you will never fully understand what just happened. I am the rabbi of a conservative Jewish congregation. What you have just shared runs counter to everything I have taught and that we believe. But when I look into your eyes, I see truth. I see that Christ enabled you to forgive the man. I see that Christ healed you."

The rabbi then asked, "Do you ever tell your story to Jewish congregations?"

Paula said, "Sir, because my story is about forgiveness and Christ. . . ."

"Ah, yes," the rabbi replied. "The invitations wouldn't be forthcoming. But if you were asked, would you consider sharing your perspective with them?"

And ever-respectful Paula replied to the rabbi, "Yes, sir, I would be honored."

∾∾o∾

We can learn to identify The Genuine. To do this, of course, means that we have to be awake and paying attention. We cannot be Slothful. The indifferent and apathetic will not recognize the Voice of God because they won't care enough to do so.

∾o∾

Paula says that on the way home what happened hit her, and she had to pull over to the side of the road to cry. The rabbi later told Paula that he went home, told the story to his wife, and he, too, cried. Paula subsequently enrolled in the rabbi's study group of the Hebrew Bible with his congregation. One evening when she went to the class, the rabbi met her at the door and said, "Paula, remember how I asked you whether, given the invitation, you would share your perspective?" Paula indeed remembered. The rabbi said, "Tonight is the night I would like to call on you." And the rabbi introduced her, and Paula was invited to share something of her faith in Jesus Christ, healing, and the forgiveness of sins.

When I heard Paula tell this story, she said, "All of his life, this rabbi had been training himself to hear the Voice of God. And when God was speaking to him, he recognized the Voice."

Whenever I have invited Paula to speak in the church I am serving, when people ask me why they should take time to hear her, I tell them that every time I have been in Paula's presence, I have experienced the Presence of God and heard God's Voice. Paula's story about her friend the rabbi is one of those treasures that complements what Dallas Willard teaches us. In both Paula's demeanor and her words, as well as the rabbi's reflections, I somehow sense the weight of God's compelling authority. The rabbi found Paula's words to be self-authenticating. The spirit in which she spoke was one of tremendous respect, gentleness, and kindness. And her message — what Dallas Willard calls the "contents" — are at the heart of Jesus' grace, which delivers us and makes forgiveness possible.

One of the things that I find so compelling in this story is the rabbi's willingness to reflect, even when his reflections were not entirely in sync with his own orientation and tradition. In that sense, Paula's rabbi was listening not so much as analyst or scholar; he was listening with the heart of a child. He was full of wonder and curiosity. And wonder and curiosity lie close to the heart of reflection.

I wish I could say that I have developed the discipline and perseverance to listen to God each and every moment. I have yet to develop that level of concentration. And there doesn't seem to be much danger that this will happen soon! I am still learning. I probably always will be. Being human, I still make mistakes. Being fallen, I still sin. But I have found great encouragement from Richard Rohr — Franciscan priest, retreat leader, and teacher of contemplative prayer — when he has said that God blesses what we are trying to say yes to.

# LIVING IN REFLECTION

*All those things that had formerly been vague, colorless, seen from the outside . . . became suddenly for me living, interesting, inspiring. Each man became inestimably precious in my eyes.*

— André Trocmé, in Philip Hallie, *Lest Innocent Blood Be Shed*

**W**ALKER PERCY once wrote, "You can get all As and still flunk life." His insight came to mind when I pondered what it would take to be completely (or sufficiently) rid of Sloth. If Sloth results from a militant indifference and willful apathy that anesthetizes us to matters of import, and sustained, thoughtful reflection is the opposite of Sloth, then how do I live a life of reflection without getting stuck in what we sometimes call "morbid introspection"? It occurred to me that a discipline of reflection is far more than a mere mental exercise. I never want to suggest that following Christ involves *mere* reflection, any more than I'd want to suggest that it has to do with mere fasting, mere solitude, or mere service.

A person can have a wealth of knowledge. It can be accurate and true. A person can pass all of his or her exams. But none of this guarantees our living a transformed life. I could, for example, take a class in moral reasoning, earn an A for the class, but still not be a very nice person. What does it look like to *live* in reflection? How does one whom God transforms through meaningful reflection live?

It is well known that during the Holocaust, Adolf Hitler and his death camps exterminated six and a half million Jews. His goal was to extinguish the entire race of God's chosen people. Millions of Jews reached out to others and asked for help. I suspect that most of the people from whom the Jews sought help were followers of Christ. And I would guess that a significant number of them knew the Holocaust to be wrong, but they still refused to help. Did their Sloth and indifference override their moral knowledge? I do not know the answer to this, and I am not sure it is my place to decide.

What I have learned, on the other hand, is that some people who reflected on the plight of the Jews did offer help at great risk to their own lives. Doing so required courage. To read their stories is to discover that those who aided the Jews were as far from being indifferent as one can imagine. I think the story that has made the biggest impact on my life is the story of Pastor André Trocmé, who led a small Huguenot village in southern France, called Le Chambon, to save five thousand Jews, most of whom were children. Under the influence of Pastor Trocmé's gracious leadership, the people of Le Chambon welcomed the Jews with open arms. Trocmé hid the refugees in the homes of his parish members. He alone knew where each refugee was secreted. This meant that if anyone who provided refuge was arrested, they would not be able to divulge the whereabouts of other refugees.

One of the many reasons that Trocmé's story is important is that he was one of the exceptions in Europe during the Holocaust. Unlike most others, he did not turn a blind eye on the Jews. Trocmé was not indifferent and uncaring. When they came, fleeing Hitler, seeking help, simply put, he helped. *Trocmé believed that to help is better than to harm, and his response to the Jews reflected his belief.* And Trocmé believed that he should love not only the Jews, but also his enemies. Many of us believe in this ideal. Trocmé actually followed through. At one point, he and his wife, Magda, invited André's arresting officers to have dinner with them. This happened during André's arrest. This piqued my curiosity. How was it that André Trocmé not only *thought* he should love his enemies and help those who needed his help but *actually did both* — with goodness aforethought?

Philip Hallie published an extraordinary book about Trocmé and his family entitled *Lest Innocent Blood Be Shed*. One of the reasons I find Hallie's book to be so important is that he reports Trocmé's reflections on formative turning points in his life that shaped Trocmé's beliefs and character, leading him actually to help.

Two of Trocmé's formative events took place during his childhood. The first happened when he was ten years old. The Trocmé family was out for a Sunday drive. André's father was overcome with what today we would call "road rage." The family sedan, which André's father was driving, was behind a small jalopy that had pulled in front of the Trocmé car when they were stopped at a railroad crossing. After the train passed, the driver of the jalopy spun his wheels, throwing dirt and pebbles on the Trocmé sedan, and surged ahead. André's father, Paul, became enraged. He then accelerated the family car toward the jalopy. The driver of the jalopy reacted by positioning his car in the center of the road as they were going downhill, preventing Paul from passing. Trocmé refused to slow down. Finally, he had to swerve to avoid hitting the jalopy. The Trocmé sedan rolled. Trocmé's mother was thrown from the car. She lay still, with her legs slightly apart and blood trickling from her mouth. Three days later, the hospital physician pronounced her dead.

When Paul Trocmé broke the news to his boys, he shouted, "I killed her! I killed her!" Young André threw his arms around his father and pleaded with him never to drive again. André's older brother, Robert, also embraced their father.

André reported to Philip Hallie that because of his mother, the Trocmé home had been "deep as a cradle." André's mother had made beautiful music. She had swept the boys up in her arms and hugged and kissed them. Until she died, André had felt himself to be a part of his mother. Her death was the first death he experienced; with her loss, death became real for him.

André responded to his mother's death with deep, sustained reflection. When he did so, he discovered the sheer, unqualified preciousness of life. The preciousness of his mother's life extended to others: he became aware of the infinite preciousness of every human being.

At the same time, André reflected on his need lovingly to forgive his mother's killer. Why? Among other things, his mother's killer was also his own father. And as André reflected, he recognized that only forgiveness could heal the family's brokenness and restore its wholeness. It was in reflection that André came to this awareness.

The other formative event from Trocmé's childhood took place during World War I. Young André came home one day to discover that a German soldier was being quartered in the Trocmé home. The first time André met this soldier, the man offered Trocmé some black potato bread. André refused the offer, declaring the soldier to be an enemy who was out to kill André's brother who was fighting Germans in the French army. The man told André that he would never kill André's brother because he was a Christian, a conscientious objector, and a pacifist. This was the first conscientious objector André had met. What stunned him was that this man was an "enemy" who refused to kill anyone in the army in which his own brother fought.

Reflecting on these two experiences, Trocmé developed beliefs that were his rock: all life is precious, do no harm, and prevent others from doing harm.

Hallie reports another formative experience of Trocmé's that occurred during his early adulthood and involved members of his parish and God. Trocmé was a young pastor. He had organized his parish into house Bible studies, one of which consisted of a group of men who were struggling with poor working conditions, poverty, and alcoholism. The group was called "The Men's Circle." On one particular evening at their Bible study, the men were discussing a book whose author argued that Jesus was a myth invented by the apostle Paul. André posed a question to the group, compelling each of them to reflect: "If Jesus really walked upon this earth, why do we keep treating him as if he were a disembodied, impossibly idealistic ethical theory? If he was a real man, then the Sermon on the Mount was made for people on this earth, and if he existed, God has shown us in flesh and blood what goodness is for flesh-and-blood people." Trocmé's words were spontaneous. He did not know that he was going to respond to the book in this way. He had not planned this speech, and he spoke calmly. What followed his remarks surprised him as much as it did the men in the group. Each man fell to his knees and confessed his sins to God, aloud, in the group's hearing. When their prayers were concluded, the men rose to their feet. Their eyes were shining. The defensiveness with which the men had treated each other dissolved. The pride with which they had regarded others was gone. They were aware that the Spirit of God was filling them. Together, they enjoyed what they recognized as an awakening — what Trocmé called "a spiritual springtime." "All those things that had formerly been vague, colorless, seen from the outside ... became suddenly for me living, interesting, inspiring. Each man became inestimably precious in my eyes."

Trocmé told Hallie that this experience was not mere mystical ecstasy. Reflecting their direct experience of the Presence of God, the men responded by serving God and his children. This meant that others shared in their reflected experience of God. This completed a transformation initiated by their reflection on God's direct Presence.

Among the results for Trocmé was the completion of the belief system that fueled his conduct. His beliefs now consisted of four complementary parts: *all life is precious, do no harm, prevent others from doing harm, and practice a person-to-God piety.* These beliefs, however, were not something that Trocmé merely pondered. He didn't just sit around and think about them. He put his beliefs into action by opening his heart to God and his arms and home to others. This included both the Jews who came to his village seeking help and those who regarded Trocmé as *the enemy* — the French Vichy police. The episode that Philip Hallie reports that stuns me the most has to do with the evening that the Vichy Police arrested Trocmé. Trocmé arrived home shortly after the police had arrived at his house. When he learned the reason for their presence, he called to his wife, "Magda, I am arrested!" She was dismayed because the suitcase that she had prepared in the event of his arrest was completely empty. They had used its contents to help others. But she would do her best to prepare a suitcase so that he would have at least some resources to survive prison; they had heard that conditions were harsh.

Magda did not care only for her husband. She also cared for the police who were standing in her home to arrest her husband. With André, she regarded them as precious life like everyone else. Since it was dinner time, Magda invited the arresting officers to join the Trocmés for dinner before taking André to prison. When Philip Hallie later asked why she extended the invitation, her response was that they were there, and it was dinner time. What else was she to do? When Hallie suggested moral praise for her hospitality, she sloughed off the praise, denying her own goodness. She simply did what she knew to be required. And what was required? Help — without condition.

André and Magda Trocmé reflected on their beliefs in the preciousness of life and a direct person-to-God piety together. Their reflections occupied much of their dialogue. Their actions also reflected their beliefs. If they were indifferent to anything, it was to the moral praise from others. Their ideas about the preciousness of life extended to refugees and "enemies" alike.

Trocmé's parishioners were so impressed by his character that they regarded Trocmé as the "Soul of Le Chambon." During the Holocaust, Trocmé would return to his home in the evening utterly exhausted from the inhumane work schedule he selflessly kept in order to give faithful refuge to others. His back hurt him frequently. Once, he was in so much pain that a member of his parish found Trocmé on the side of the road, lying on his back. The man had to put Trocmé in his cart and return him to his home. But invariably, when Trocmé arrived home, his children, thrilled to see their father, would shout, "Papa's home!" They would gather around their tired father, hug him, welcome him, and beg for their ritual game, elephant walk. One young child would stand on top of one of Trocmé's feet with his arms around his father's leg. A second child would do the same with the other foot, and his oldest son would jump up and grab Trocmé around the chest. Trocmé's daughter would climb on Trocmé's back and wrap her arms around her daddy's neck. Daddy would then walk around the house, literally carrying his family. Magda would come from the kitchen and stand in the doorway to watch, smiling over the sheer joy that Trocmé exuded for his children as he played with them.

André Trocmé carried joy within him. It came to him through a combination of thoughtful reflection and action. He was possessed by the knowledge that all life is precious, that is it better to help than to harm. André Trocmé rejoiced in the sovereign dignity of people. He *honored* the sovereign dignity in which he found so much joy.

My friend Roy uses a phrase that sticks with me. He speaks of "authentic experience." It is hard for me to imagine lives that are more authentic than those of André and Magda Trocmé. What I find remarkable is that merely to read of, ponder, and reflect on their lives is in itself a precious experience of authenticity. Brother Lawrence, in the seventeenth century, was wont to stress the importance of filling our minds with high notions of the Sovereignty of God. I wonder whether he wouldn't include the thinking and action of truly virtuous people as worthy of reflection. To experience the Trocmés, even in imagination, is to know the genuine. Their story is self-authenticating. Their actions mirror their beliefs. They are the fruit of deep reflection that has given birth to a transformed life.

# RUBY

*I close my eyes, and I think of what it must have been like for Jesus.*
— Ruby Bridges

S HE WAS ONLY six years old, but she created quite an uproar. The crowd wanted to do her bodily harm. Many wanted to kill her. Fortunately, U.S. marshals were there to protect her. They thought that they might have to draw their firearms.

Why all the commotion? The crowd was upset simply because she was there. If they didn't want her dead, they surely wanted her somewhere else.

What did this girl then do to cause a furor? She stopped and apparently said something to the crowd. How dare she! The crowd responded to the six-year-old with rage.

The year was 1960. The place was New Orleans. The courts had ordered the desegregation of the schools. A woman named Charlene Bridges was asked if she would give consent for her six-year-old daughter, Ruby, to become the first black child to attend France Elementary School. After prayerful reflection Charlene Bridges agreed. She sensed that God was calling the Bridges family to serve the cause of justice in this particular way. Charlene Bridges gave her permission, and she impressed upon her daughter the importance of what she would be doing.

The admission of a black child into France Elementary School so provoked the ire of the white people that they boycotted the school and kept their own children home. The result was that Ruby Bridges was the only child to attend that school that year. But the boycott was not the only method that the white people used to protest integration. Each day as Ruby walked into the school, a mob of white people stood there, outside the school, shouting obscenities, threatening Ruby, and calling for her death. According to Robert Coles, this lasted for the entire school year. Sometimes, there were as many as a thousand people in the crowd. This was the reason for the presence of U.S. marshals. They had to escort Ruby to ensure her safety.

Ruby Bridges's situation came to the attention of Robert Coles, a pediatric psychiatrist at Harvard. While devoting his life to understanding young people medically, Coles has also gotten to know children as people — fellow human beings. Robert Coles has been both physician and friend to many children.

Coles learned of the disturbance that Ruby had caused on the day she had paused in front of the angry mob. Curiosity and professional interest led Coles to investigate. He wanted to meet Ruby Bridges.

As Coles was getting to know Ruby, he asked her about the incident when she had stopped and apparently spoken to the crowd. Ruby told him that she had stopped to pray. He asked her why. She told him that each morning she said her prayers. This always included praying for the crowd. On the day in question, when Ruby saw the crowd, she suddenly remembered that she hadn't said her prayers that morning. As U.S. marshals escorted Ruby to school, she stopped in her tracks, right then and there, and said her prayers.

Coles asked Ruby what she prayed for for the crowd. Her answer stunned him: "Please, please, God, try to forgive those people because they don't know what they're doing."

What disarmed Coles was realizing that this prayer came from the lips of a child whose life was in danger. And it was a prayer for the very people who were terrorizing her at the very moment she was most in danger. This prayer came not just from a six-year-old child; it came from a child who was, as we would say today, *at risk*. Coles learned that risk pervaded Ruby's entire life: "Talk about at-risk young people. This was a family at risk. Utterly at risk. Socially at risk. Racially at risk. Educationally at risk. Culturally at risk. Economically at risk. You name the variable or adjective, they possessed it."

What might happen if our churches were to become — once again — a community in reflection?

In spite of the risk, Ruby's strength was astonishing. And Coles wanted to learn about the source of Ruby Bridges's strength of character. What kind of support did she receive? What had built Ruby's astonishing character?

Coles found the answer in Ruby's church. The Bridges family went to church together in New Orleans every Sunday. Coles recognized that if he were to understand Ruby, he would have to visit Ruby's church. He discovered right away that this was not an air-conditioned church. The New Orleans heat and humidity stifled him. Nor was it the kind of church that efficiently wrapped up their worship in about an hour. This was a hard-praying church — a church of witnessing, exhorting, responding, exclaiming, and testifying. These were people who knew their Bibles. They knew all about Isaiah. They knew about Jeremiah. And they knew Jesus Christ. Moreover, the people knew them *as a congregation*. And this included Ruby. She not only knew the stories of Jesus, she knew that her church — of which she was an essential part — was connected to those stories.

Ruby's church was a congregation *in reflection*. Each week, they drew into their worship both stories from the Bible and the circumstances they themselves were currently facing. With this background, Ruby consciously considered both the stories of Jesus and the situation she faced. She learned to ponder how her own situation resembled what Jesus himself went through.

Coles asked Ruby to elaborate on the prayer that she prayed for the crowd that so hated her. Ruby responded, "You know when Jesus was in trouble, there was a big mob there. And they were ready to hurt him. And that's what he said. And I try to say the same thing."

Coles asked, "Do you always believe that?"

Ruby confessed her struggle to sustain her faith: "No, I don't always believe that, but I try to." When Coles pushed her for further elaboration, she described her *reflections:* "I close my eyes, and I think of what it must have been like for Jesus."

Ruby's church had taught her how her own trials *reflected* circumstances that Jesus himself faced. They also helped Ruby see that Jesus' circumstances and his response to those circumstances were *defining occasions;* they were *sacred.* The word "sacred" may not have been a part of Ruby's vocabulary, but it was something that she knew. Jesus, his circumstances, and his response resonated inside of Ruby. She came to know Jesus; Ruby came to know him in both his circumstances and her own. She recognized that one circumstance reflected the other.

WHY WAS Ruby Bridges's church so effective? As I pondered this question, I wondered whether their way of worshiping —

with reflection at the heart of their experience — was not a fully human act. Robert Coles recognized that we humans love to wonder about things. Curiosity and wonder in some respects define us as human. We are *naturally* curious. We love to figure things out. We are deeply satisfied when a mystery is fully solved. We treasure those precious moments when we suddenly find ourselves exclaiming *aha!*

Isn't this why we find reflection to be so rewarding? And did not Ruby's church strengthen her own capacity to wonder as they worshiped and reflected together?

Perhaps without realizing they had done so, did not the church confer upon Ruby a consciousness that was fully awake? And were they not themselves free from Sloth? Not only were they not at all indifferent to things that matter, they were vitally interested in God, the stories of the Bible, the circumstances that they faced, and the preciousness and dignity of Ruby herself.

What might happen if our churches were to become — once again — a community in reflection? What if we were to bring to our gatherings both the circumstances in which we find ourselves and what William Faulkner called the "old verities" — perhaps a story Jesus told, or perhaps Jesus himself, crucified and raised from the dead? Imagine our wondering *together* what God is saying to us, in us, and through us. I once sat with a group in our church. We asked a question: What is God's will for our congregation? What is God calling us to accomplish together? The group sat in silence, listening for an answer. We then shared what we heard. We limited ourselves to expressing what we heard as either a verse of Scripture or a line from a hymn. There were common threads to what we experienced. After sharing what we heard or imagined God said to us, we began a quiet, reflective dialogue. We worked at keeping a focus — reflecting together on what we thought God was saying to us, at that moment. We imagined what God might want to emerge in and through us.

I believe that if we, in our congregations, spend ample time reflecting together on what God is saying to us, what God wants to emerge, then God will join our reflections. I also believe that when we are a community of reflection, we become more fully human.

# Love Bids Us
# Welcome

*It was during one of these recitations that ... Christ himself came down and took possession of me.*

— Simone Weil, *Waiting for God*

HER HEADACHES WERE GRUELING. Each sound that she heard felt like a blow to her head. How does one cope with such pain? Simone Weil did so by concentrating on, repeating, and reflecting on a poem.

The year was 1938. She was spending Palm Sunday through Easter Tuesday enjoying all the worship services. These ten days are known as Solesmes.

To cope with the pain, Simone Weil repeated a poem by the metaphysical poet George Herbert.

Love bade me welcome: yet my soul drew back,
    Guiltie of lust and sinne.
But quick-ey'd Love, observing me grow slack
    From my first entrance in,
Drew nearer to me, sweetly questioning,
    If I lack'd any thing.

A guest, I answer'd, worthy to be here:
    Love said, You shall be he.

155

I the unkinde, ungrateful? Ah my deare,
    I cannot look on thee.
Love took my hand, and smiling did reply,
    Who made the eyes but I?

Truth Lord, but I have marr'd them: let my shame
    Go where it doth deserve.
And know you not, sayes Love, who bore the blame?
    My deare, then I will serve.
You must sit down, says Love, and taste my meat:
    So I did sit and eat.

Simone Weil wrote that by concentrating solely on this poem, she "was able to rise above this wretched flesh, to leave it to suffer by itself, heaped up in a corner, and to find a pure and perfect joy in the unimaginable beauty of the chanting and the words." As she clung to all of the tenderness that this poem enshrines, something happened: "Christ himself came down and took possession of me." Her knowing Christ was direct — *person to person.*

Commenting on her experience, Weil writes that she had always been rather put off by the miracles in the Gospel. Moreover, she had not read of the encounters with Christ that the mystics enjoyed. Subsequent to being possessed by Christ, she reflected that God had prevented her from reading the mystics so it would be evident to her that she had not invented this experience. And her distaste for the miracles all the more underscored the authenticity of her knowing Christ directly.

What happened to Simone Weil was as extraordinary as it was simple. In the midst of excruciating pain, she found an object *worthy of her attention.* She discovered something of self-evident importance for her reflection. It was God's Love for her. The vehicle by which that Love entered her was the poem.

When she made the Love of Christ the sole object of her reflection, Christ found her. She discovered herself to be welcome. Christ was tender and hospitable. He became her joy.

∽o∾

St. Thomas Aquinas suggests that Sloth is *sadness in the face of spiritual good.* I like his explanation both because it is clear, and because it rings true.

∾o∽

When Evelyn Waugh, an English author, wrote on the Deadly Sin of Sloth, he said that theologians sometimes employ the technical term *acedia,* which suggests apathy or boredom. But Waugh added, "There is no true classical term for this state, not because it was unknown to the ancients, but because it was too commonplace to require identification." The Deadly Sin of Pride is classically described by the Greek word *hubris,* which has to do with an arrogant self-confidence that is also self-centered and blind. Though lacking a classical definition, numerous theologians have discussed Sloth. St. Thomas Aquinas, for example, suggests that Sloth is *sadness in the face of spiritual good.* I like his explanation both because it is clear, and because it rings true.

Evelyn Waugh also seems to understand that we as individuals need to be able to identify Sloth, to recognize it and take responsibility for its removal from our lives. Taking responsibility does not mean that we don't need the grace of God to remove Sloth. Taking responsibility means first *recognizing* Sloth so God can help us conquer Sloth and steadily move to better paths through reflection.

Simone Weil had much to feel sorry about. Had she become dejected, had she given up in despair, would we have criticized her? Would we have judged her? To the contrary, we probably would have found any criticism to be harsh, if not cruel.

However, in spite of her condition and in the midst of her pain, Simone Weil concentrated and reflected on the Love of God for her. She willingly focused on the Supreme Good, without self-pity, discouragement, sadness, or despair. Free of Sloth, in the face of spiritual good she found Love.

Love draws near to each of us. Is there reason to draw back?

Love seeks. Are we pushing Love away?

Our eyes are closed, maybe blind. But Love ever gently nudges, offering the gift of sight. Is anything more precious?

We often are guilty of Sloth. Will we let that become our excuse for not loving? Love is eager that we be released and free — free to love.

Love offers not crumbs, but a banquet. Love desires that we sit and eat — not tomorrow, not even later in the day, but right here, right now.

Love seeks to become our Joy.

This is it!

# THE OTHER SIX
## DEADLY SINS

I WAS CUDGELING MY BRAIN. I thought I remembered someone having written something to the effect that *Sloth not
only poisons our virtues, but our vices as well.* Alas! My memory was faulty. The statement wasn't about Sloth; it was about
Pride. G. K. Chesterton gets the credit: "Pride is a poison so
very poisonous that it not only poisons the virtues; it even
poisons the other vices." He makes this statement in an essay
entitled, "If I Had Only One Sermon to Preach."

But in spite of my faulty memory, I still wondered whether
Sloth doesn't somehow poison the other six Deadly Sins —
Pride, Envy, Wrath, Avarice, Gluttony, and Lust. What would
this mean? It would mean that our spirits and character were
so indifferent, so debilitated by despair, that we completely ignored the impact and consequences of the other six Deadly
Sins, or we became possessed by a morbid, sad, helpless doubt
over God's ability and willingness to save us from all Seven
Deadly Sins.

What are the other six Deadly Sins?

Pride means making oneself the center of the universe.
When possessed by Pride, we make our own lives the criterion
and standard for all judgments and decisions. We also spend
much of our time concealing just how much we look down on
others.

Envy means weeping when others rejoice and rejoicing when others weep. When we are envious, we can't stand for something good to happen to someone else. We also secretly rejoice when others suffer disaster or tragedy.

Wrath means willing harm to another person. When filled with Wrath, we will actually cause or allow someone else to be harmed. This is often because we have no sense of another person's dignity and preciousness.

Avarice refers to the love of money. When possessed by this sin, we worship our own purchasing power, along with our possessions.

Gluttony refers to the love of eating. Perhaps the love of consuming would be more accurate. Gluttony can also include the love of drinking, the love of drugs, and the love of smoking.

Lust refers to the love of sex and the love of bodies. This is significantly different from the love for a person. And like Gluttony, Lust includes the hunger and thirst for personal stimulation.

What happens when Sloth poisons the other six Deadly Sins? We become indifferent to them. We may deny their existence. We may deny their significance. Or we may come to rejoice in these sins for their own sake and even their destructiveness. And if Sloth turns into despair, we may desperately seek relief from the other Deadly Sins, but become debilitated by doubts over God's willingness to deliver us into the world of God's sovereign will and joy.

# DEEPENING
# REFLECTIONS

Paula D'Arcy, *A New Set of Eyes* and *Seeking with All My Heart*.
Paula's books help us begin to live in the present moment, where we can meet the hidden God, sometimes in places we least expect.

Dallas Willard, *Hearing God*.
He gives clear directions for recognizing God's voice in both one's prayer life and everyday life.

Richard Rohr, *Everything Belongs*.
This book helps us learn how to recognize and accept all that appears before us in life as essential to living with God.

Os Guinness, *Long Journey Home* and *The Call*.
Os teaches us to set our lives in the larger world of the history of life as a journey. He shows us how to hear God's call in the whole of our lives.

David Aikman, *Great Souls*.
This former senior correspondent for *Time* magazine reflects on some of the "saints" of modern times, including Mother Teresa and Aleksandr Solzhenitsyn.

# Acknowledgments

ALTHOUGH AN AUTHOR spends many hours in solitude, writing a book is not something we do alone. It requires a team. And I take great pleasure in offering heartfelt gratitude to people who are a part of that team and have encouraged and supported me during the preparation of this book. I would like to begin with Roy M. Carlisle, Senior Editor of The Crossroad Publishing Company and Crossroad Carlisle Books. Roy is the captain of the team. I had the good fortune to meet Roy through our mutual friend, Paula D'Arcy. Thanks to her, Roy and I grew to enjoy a creative, prayerful partnership. He is at once editor, mentor, and friend. Roy is as gracious as he is uncompromising. Roy makes writing a joy because with his leadership, it is always an adventure in learning. He has a way of asking questions that allow entirely new pathways to emerge in my reflections. Roy is an inspiration because he believes so deeply in what he is doing. And because he brings love, knowledge, experience, and deep commitment to our dialogue, collaborating with him is pure joy. I not only thank him, I thank God that this is the beginning of a working relationship.

Shirley Coe is also a key player on the team. Her copy-editing is so astute that I have received an education in the English language from her. John Eagleson reviewed the proofs with great skill and care.

Many thanks to the rest of the team at the Crossroad Publishing Company for their extraordinary work.

There are other mentors whom I wish to thank. Paula D'Arcy is my mentor in prayer. I still struggle to know God directly. Any success I enjoy is because of her teaching, example, and patient prayerfulness. Paula's knowing God is ever-present as I write and as Roy and I dialogue.

The person who first awakened me to the importance of understanding the Seven Deadly Sins is Os Guinness, Senior Fellow of the Trinity Forum in Washington, D.C. Os is my intellectual mentor and inspiration. Everything that I write and teach is influenced by his books, teaching, and friendship.

In the same vein, I want to thank my colleagues at First United Methodist Church of San Diego — Jim Standiford, Molly Vetter, Randy Newton, Djalma Araujo, Peggy Goochéy, and Tom Hamilton. They are partners in reflection. That they endure and even indulge my ideas is evidence of the grace of God. My administrative assistant at First Church is Demmie Divine. She is a constant cheerleader who always helps me set aside time for study, reflection, teaching, and writing. Demmie is also a great friend.

There are also two schools of learning associated with First Church to which I owe gratitude — the San Diego School of Christian Studies and the Inklings. Most of what appears in this book they have reflected upon with me in classes and dialogues that I have taught or led. They are lifelong learners from whom I have gained far more than I have offered. I am honored to call them fellow students and friends. I also wish to thank the Koinonia Class of First Church. I have taught much of this material in their class. Their enthusiasm for learning is matched by their zest for life. They are remarkable friends.

The University United Methodist Church of Las Vegas also invited me to teach much of this material in seminars. This church has enriched both my life and these pages, and I am grateful.

I also wish to thank Peter Francis, Warden of St. Deiniol's Residential Theological Library in Wales, along with his gracious staff. I wrote the first draft of this manuscript at St. Deiniol's. It is a writer's paradise.

My friend Shirley Leggett has spent countless hours proofreading for me. Moreover, her sharp eye has identified many places where I have been less than clear. This manuscript has benefited immeasurably from her keen attention and commitment.

Finally, I thank my family — Nancy, Jaime, and David. With them, I have ever lived in reflection. Although many have contributed to my growth, none has done more so than my family. First and last, they are my greatest supporters, teachers, and cheerleaders. The grace wherewith they have loved me cannot begin to be measured. I can only wish that my gratitude for them will in some measure do justice to their remarkable and extraordinary love.

# ABOUT THE AUTHOR

John N. Blackwell is a United Methodist pastor who was born and raised in San Diego. After serving churches in Arizona and Nevada, he returned to his hometown, where he serves as minister of discipleship at First United Methodist Church of San Diego. John is also dean and senior fellow of the San Diego School of Christian Studies, the purpose of which is to offer seminary-level education for laity. He is also a faculty member in the department of philosophy and religion at Point Loma University. John is founder of the Inklings, a group of youth and college students who meet for dialogue and reflection on classics of literature.

For over twenty-five years, John has been a retreat leader for people of all ages and a speaker at various conferences. He also has a vital interest in higher education and campus ministry.

John received his education at San Diego State University, Claremont School of Theology, and Arizona State University, from which he earned a PhD in cultural anthropology. John is the author of *The Passion as Story* and several scholarly articles.

John and his wife, Nancy, make their home in the San Diego area of California. They have two adult children, Jaime and David. John enjoys music, reading, writing, rose gardening, and travel.